DOCUMENTS DIVISION

6 00 016000 9   TELEPEN

KU-181-665

WORLD BANK STAFF OCCASIONAL PAPERS NUMBER SEVENTEEN

This paper may not be quoted as representing the view of the Bank and its affiliated organizations. They do not accept responsibility for its accuracy or completeness.

WORLD BANK STAFF OCCASIONAL PAPERS NUMBER SEVENTEEN

Edited by
Ian Bowen

Kenji Takeuchi

Tropical Hardwood Trade in the Asia-Pacific Region

Distributed by The Johns Hopkins University Press
Baltimore and London

Copyright © 1974 by the International Bank for
Reconstruction and Development

All rights reserved
Manufactured in the United States of America

Library of Congress Catalog Card Number 74-4214
ISBN 0-8018-1627-0

Library of Congress Cataloging in Publication data will
be found on the last printed page of this book.

Foreword

I would like to explain *why* the World Bank Group does research work, and why it publishes it. We feel an obligation to look beyond the projects we help to finance toward the whole resource allocation of an economy, and the effectiveness of the use of those resources. Our major concern, in dealings with member countries, is that all scarce resources, including capital, skilled labor, enterprise and know-how, should be used to their best advantage. We want to see policies that encourage appropriate increases in the supply of savings, whether domestic or international. Finally, we are required by our Articles, as well as by inclination, to use objective economic criteria in all our judgments.

These are our preoccupations, and these, one way or another, are the subjects of most of our research work. Clearly, they are also the proper concern of anyone who is interested in promoting development, and so we seek to make our research papers widely available. In doing so, we have to take the risk of being misunderstood. Although these studies are published by the Bank, the views expressed and the methods explored should not necessarily be considered to represent the Bank's views or policies. Rather they are offered as a modest contribution to the great discussion on how to advance the economic development of the underdeveloped world.

ROBERT S. MCNAMARA
President
International Bank for
Reconstruction and Development

Table of Contents

FOREWORD v

LIST OF TABLES ix

GLOSSARY xi

PREFACE. xiii

SUMMARY xv

I.   TOWARD A REGIONAL TIMBER POLICY   3
    The Present Pattern of Tropical Hardwood Trade
        in the Asia-Pacific Region.   4
    Demand, Supply, and Price Outlook for Tropical
        Hardwood in the Asia-Pacific Region   5
    Wood Processing: An Ideal Vehicle of Industrial
        Growth in the Philippines, Malaysia, and Indonesia   7
    Problems in the Growth of Processed Wood Exports
        from the Log-Producing Countries   9
    A Strategy for Accelerating the Growth of Processed
        Wood Exports from the Log-Producing Countries.   10
    Need for Better Control of Timber Resources:
        A Long-Term Forestry Policy.   14
        Policy Implications   15

II. TRENDS IN WORLD WOOD ECONOMY   17
    Trends in the Production and Consumption of Forest
        Products.   17
    Demand Prospects for Wood   22
    Trends in World Trade in Forest Products   22

III. SOURCES OF TROPICAL HARDWOOD   27
    Africa.   30
    Latin America   33
    The Asia-Pacific Region.   34

IV. MARKETS FOR TROPICAL HARDWOOD: TRENDS
     AND PROSPECTS.   37
       The Growth of Trade in Processed Tropical Hardwood . . .   40
       Demand in the United States   42
       Demand in Japan   46
       Demand in Europe   50
       World Demand Prospects   52
V.   PRICE TRENDS AND OUTLOOK FOR TROPICAL
     HARDWOOD IN THE ASIA-PACIFIC REGION   53
       Price Trends   53
       Price Outlook   57
ANNEX 1: Projected Export Earnings from Timber of the
          Philippines, Malaysia, and Indonesia, 1980   62
ANNEX 2: Import Duties on Tropical Wood Products in
          Developed Countries.   64
ANNEX 3: Tropical Timber Bureau   68
STATISTICAL APPENDIX: Tables A.1–A.19   69
REFERENCES   86

List of Tables

2.1 Change in Recorded World Use of Wood and Wood Products, 1950-52 to 1969

2.2 World Production (Consumption) of Logs by Specie Groups, 1954-56, 1964-66, and 1968

2.3 World Requirements (in Roundwood Equivalent) of Wood and Wood Products, 1962, and Projections to 1975, 1980, and 1985

2.4 World Consumption of Selected Forest Products—Past Trends (1954-68) and Projections (1975, 1980, 1985)

2.5 Trade of Major Forest Products in 1968, World and Economic Classes

3.1 World's Hardwood Forest Resources

3.2 Tropical Hardwood: Exports of Logs and Processed Products as Compared with Production of Logs, by Region, 1955 and 1968

3.3 Exports of Tropical Hardwood Logs by Selected Countries, 1954, 1957, 1960, 1963, and 1965-71

4.1 Projected Demand for Tropical Hardwood, by Major Areas, up to 1985

4.2 Exports of Tropical Hardwood Sawnwood by Selected Countries, by Destination, 1968

4.3 Direction of Trade in Hardwood Plywood, Selected Exporting Areas, by Destination, 1969

4.4 Exports of Veneer Sheets (All Species) by Developing Countries, 1968

4.5 U.S. Imports of Hardwood Plywood, by Country of Origin, 1955-72

4.6 Japan's Imports of Logs, by Geographical Sources, and by Species, 1954-72

4.7 Japan's Imports of Processed Tropical Hardwood, 1961-65, 1966-71

4.8 Japan: Projected Domestic Supply of and Total Demand and Import Demand for Industrial Wood (All Species), 1980 and 1981

4.9 Europe: Forest Products Balance, 1950-70, and Estimates, 1980-2000

5.1 Export and Import Unit Values of Logs in World Trade, 1960-70

5.2 C.i.f. Unit Values of Lauan and Apitong Logs Imported by Japan, by Country of Origin, 1953-72

ANNEX TABLES

1.1 Estimated Growth of Timber Exports from the Philippines, Malaysia, and Indonesia, 1968 and 1980

2.1 Tariff Rates on Selected Forest Products in Japan

2.2 U.S. Tariff Rates on Selected Forest Products

2.3 EEC Common Tariffs on Selected Forest Products

2.4 U.K. External Tariffs on Selected Forest Products, Prior to Joining the EEC

STATISTICAL APPENDIX TABLES

For a list of Tables A.1–A.19, see page 69.

Glossary

BTN	Brussels Tariff Nomenclature
c.i.f.	Cost, insurance and freight
CPEs	Centrally Planned Economy Countries
f.o.b.	Free on board
Hardwood	Broadleaved species, nonconifers
Logs	A shorthand notation for sawlogs, veneerlogs, and logs for sleepers
Sleepers	Railroad sleepers or ties
SITC	Standard Industrial Trade Classification
Softwood	Coniferous species, conifers
Tropical Africa	The continent excluding South Africa
Tropical Asia-Pacific Region	Includes countries in South Asia, Southeast Asia and developing Oceania; excludes Japan, Korea, Taiwan, Australia, and New Zealand
Tropical Latin America	Central and south continent excluding Argentina, Chile, and Uruguay but including the Caribbean countries

Organizations

ASEAN	Association of Southeast Asian Nations
ECA	UN Economic Commission for Africa
ECE	UN Economic Committee for Europe
ECLA	UN Economic Commission for Latin America
EEC	European Economic Community (here, unless otherwise noted, EEC refers to The Six, i.e., France, Federal Republic of Germany, The Netherlands, Italy, Belgium, and Luxembourg)
FAO	UN Food and Agriculture Organization

GATT	General Agreement on Tariffs and Trade
IBRD	International Bank for Reconstruction and Development
IMF	International Monetary Fund
ITC	GATT International Trade Center
OECD	Organization for Economic Cooperation and Development
UNCTAD	UN Conference on Trade and Development
UNDP	UN Development Program
UNIDO	UN Industrial Development Organization

Measurement

BF	board feet; 1,000 BF of roundwood $= 4.53$ m^3(r); 1,000 BF of sawnwood $= 2.36$ m^3(s)
ha.	hectare; 1 ha. $= 2.47$ acres
m^3(r)	cubic meters of roundwood
m^3(s)	cubic meters of sawnwood
m^{3}WRME	wood raw material equivalent, including roundwood equivalent of wood residues consumed in the production of particle board, fiberboard, and wood pulp

Preface

The author is indebted to past and present colleagues in the Commodities and Export Projections Division of the World Bank for their encouragement in the course of preparing this paper. Thanks are due to Messrs. R.D.H. Rowe, A.S. Tarnawiecki, B. Varon, and M.R. Oberdorfer of the World Bank Group; S.L. Pringle and Theo Erfurth of the FAO Forestry Department; T.J. Peck of the FAO/ECE Timber Division; F. Schmithusen and H.M. Gregersen, forestry consultants to the World Bank Group; and D. Hair of the U.S. Forest Service for their helpful comments on earlier drafts. The author also benefited from a number of individuals and organizations consulted during field visits to the Asia-Pacific region in the spring of 1972. Statistical computations and the preparation of tables by Mrs. Helen Bothwell and Mrs. J.G.S. Chhabra are gratefully acknowledged. Ultimately, of course, views and conclusions expressed in the paper are the sole responsibility of the author.

KENJI TAKEUCHI

Summary

The main purpose of this paper is to highlight some policy issues facing tropical hardwood trade in the Asia-Pacific region. The paper attempts to answer three questions which are frequently posed in relation to this region:

How can log-exporting countries accelerate the development of forest industries and the growth of processed wood exports?

Is it possible for the major log-exporting developing countries in the region to increase their earnings from log exports through concerted action? A corollary question is: If the major log-exporting LDCs in the region should jointly try to discourage the exports of logs for the purpose of encouraging domestic processing, will they as a group suffer a loss, or reap a gain, in their earnings from log exports in the short run?

What should be the long-term targets in the management of forest resources in the Asia-Pacific region?

Tropical hardwood resources offer excellent opportunities for the economic development of the Asia-Pacific region, since world import demand for tropical hardwood will grow at 6.0 percent to 6.5 percent per annum (in roundwood equivalent volume) during the 1970 decade and prices of logs are expected to rise markedly in the latter half of the decade. The world's three largest exporters of tropical hardwood are in the Asia-Pacific region — the Philippines, Malaysia and Indonesia — and account for two-thirds (in volume) of tropical hardwood exports.

Earnings from tropical hardwood exports, including processed products, could increase at an average annual rate of 11 percent to 12 percent during the 1970s. These figures compare to a 4 percent growth rate projected for export earnings from all agricultural commodities of developing countries, through:

Increased *volume* (in roundwood equivalent) of exports. Exports of the three main producers totalled 23.5 million $m^3(r)$ in 1968; this could increase to 43 $m^3(r)$ by 1980.

Increased average *prices* of logs. There will be a growing shortage of tropical hardwood after 1975, unless new sources of supply — forests in Papua/New Guinea, Latin America and Africa — are tapped extensively. The estimated volume of exports (total sustainable yield minus projected domestic consumption) available from traditional sources will be inadequate to meet demand from importing areas. Since the unit cost of production in new areas is likely to be substantially higher, prices are bound to rise considerably after 1975.

Increased *value* of exports by increasing the proportion of processed products (sawnwood, veneers, plywood, and so forth) from the present 15 percent to 20 percent to a possible 65 percent, while reducing the exports of logs correspondingly.

Export earnings could rise to about $1.8 billion by 1980, compared to 1968 earnings of about $500 million. Realizing this potential requires active timber development policies in the region.

Roughly three-quarters of the logs exported by the Philippines, Malaysia, and Indonesia are destined for Japan; most of the rest go to Korea, Taiwan, and Singapore, which "re-export" these logs in processed form — primarily plywood but also sawnwood and veneers. The United States has been the main market for the plywood. Thus, there are basically three types of trading partners involved: log-exporting lesser developed countries (the Philippines, Malaysia, and Indonesia), in-transit processor lesser developed countries (Korea, Taiwan, and Singapore) and developed importer-consumers (Japan and the United States).

Although the Philippines and Malaysia have well-established wood processing industries, more than 80 percent of the tropical hardwood exports are still in the form of logs. Indonesia does not have a significant processing industry. Wood processing (processing of logs into sawnwood, veneers, plywood, and so forth) is an ideal vehicle to accelerate the industrialization of these countries at the present stage of their economic development. Wood exporting is a typically weight-losing (hence freight-cost-saving) activity and a relatively labor-intensive activity; also, wood exporting requires relatively simple technology and easy-to-learn skills and provides a good opportunity to industrialize "remote areas" (outer islands) on the basis of locally available resources.

The recent change in the industrial and trade strategy of the Philippines and Indonesia from being markedly inward-looking to outward-looking will have to be developed even further if they are to realize their maximum potential foreign exchange earnings from processed wood exports. Four measures, if adopted by the log-exporting countries, could contribute to the development of wood processing industries in these countries:

Discourage the exports of logs by jointly maintaining substantial export taxes on logs.

Encourage the growth of export-oriented wood processing industries by providing incentives.

Adjust forestry concession policies so as to discourage exports of logs and encourage those of processed products.

Improve infrastructure to induce rapid growth of export-oriented wood processing industries.

Imposing export taxes raises the question of whether the exporting countries will lose in terms of total foreign exchange earnings, since they will be selling less volume although they will get a higher average price per unit. Since the price elasticity of demand for log exports of the three major Asian exporters is probably less than unity or, at worst, not much larger than unity (except in an extremely high price range), by acting jointly to discourage their own log exports, the Philippines, Malaysia, and Indonesia would probably gain — or at worst not lose much — in terms of total foreign exchange earnings from logs, while benefitting from increasing their exports of higher value processed products.

In view of the anticipated change in the pattern of tropical hardwood trade, it appears to the advantage of the developed countries to "upgrade" their wood processing industries. They should discourage primary wood processing by reducing the tariff barriers to imports of processed wood products and encourage the specialization in the most sophisticated wood products. International financial institutions should probably follow a lending program in forestry which anticipates and fosters these long-run developments in the Asia-Pacific region. Investment opportunities can be found in infrastructure (internal land and sea transportation and public utilities), primary wood processing industries (mainly in the log-producing countries, secondary wood processing industries (mainly in the in-transit processor countries, fast-growing forestry plantations, pulp and paper projects, and forestry education.

Furthermore, possible investment strategies on the part of international financial institutions aimed at opening up currently "inaccessible" tropical hardwood resources in Latin America and remote areas of Africa should be studied by these institutions, in view of the expected rising world prices of tropical hardwoods. Opening up new areas will restrain soaring prices but, since the costs of opening up these areas would be high, prices would likely stabilize at relatively high levels. The three Asian countries where costs of exploitation are much lower should be able to soak up a large part of the producers' surplus, if government policies and institutional arrangements are conducive.

Tropical Hardwood Trade in the Asia-Pacific Region

I. Toward a Regional Timber Policy

Tropical hardwood resources offer excellent opportunities for the economic development of the Asia-Pacific region. World import demand for tropical hardwood will grow at 6.0 percent to 6.5 percent per annum (in roundwood equivalent volume) during the 1970 decade. Prices of logs are expected to rise markedly in the latter half of the decade. The world's largest three exporters of tropical hardwood are in the Asia-Pacific region — the Philippines, Malaysia, and Indonesia. They currently account for two-thirds (in volume) of total exports of tropical hardwood from all producing countries. In 1968, the three countries exported about 23.5 million $m^3(r)$, worth about half a billion dollars. Hardwood exports of the three countries are likely to increase to about 43 million $m^3(r)$ per annum — estimated exportable surplus in all forms — by 1980. The export earnings from tropical hardwood of the three countries would rise to about 1.8 billion dollars by 1980 if they could increase the proportion of processed products (sawnwood, veneers, plywood, and so forth) in their exports from the current 15 percent to 20 percent to a possible 65 percent, reducing the proportion of log exports correspondingly. These proportions are based on roundwood equivalent volume. (See Annex 1.)

Export earnings from tropical hardwood (including primary processed products as well as logs) of the Philippines, Malaysia, and Indonesia could potentially increase at an average rate of 11 percent to 12 percent per annum during the 1968-1980 period as a result of increased total export volume (in roundwood equivalent), increased average prices of logs, and increased value added due to greater volume of processed wood exports. This growth rate is to be compared with a growth rate of about 4 percent

3

projected for the export earnings of developing countries from all agricultural commodities over the same period. This potential may be realized if the countries involved recognize their long-run interests and adopt appropriate policies.

The Present Pattern of Tropical Hardwood Trade in the Asia-Pacific Region

Currently, annual production of industrial wood in the developing countries in the Far East and the southwest Pacific islands (the Asia-Pacific region) is about 57 million $m^3(r)$, more than 90 percent of which is of hardwood species. The region accounts for about two-thirds of total exports of tropical hardwood from all producing areas.[1]

From the viewpoint of tropical hardwood resources, the tropical Asia-Pacific region can be broadly divided into four parts: the Dipterocarp area of mainland and insular Southeast Asia, the non-Dipterocarp area of southwest Pacific islands, teak forest areas of Burma and Thailand, and the Indian subcontinent plus Ceylon. Commercially, the Dipterocarp area is the most important of the four areas. It includes all of Indochina, the Philippines, and Malaysia as well as Indonesia west of the "Wallace Line," which separates the Malukus, Lesser Sunda Island, and West Irian from the rest of Indonesia. The non-Dipterocarp southwest Pacific islands include Indonesia east of the "Wallace line," Papua/New Guinea, the Solomon Islands, and other tropical Pacific islands. Forests in Burma and Thailand are basically Dipterocarp forests but they also contain teak resources. Burma and Thailand, along with the island of Java [Indonesia], have been the important source of teakwood exports for a number of decades. In the Indian subcontinent and Ceylon, almost all of the industrial wood produced (10 million m^3 in 1958, of which 90 percent was hardwood) is consumed domestically. This area will not become a major exporter of tropical hardwood.

Timber trade in the tropical Asia-Pacific region has been dominated by exports of logs (veneer logs, sawlogs and some logs for railroad ties) of Dipterocarpus and Shorea genera mainly from the Philippines, Malaysia, and Indonesia to Japan, Korea, Taiwan, and Singapore. These species are traded under such popular commercial names at lauans, apitongs, merantis ramin, and keruing. The dominant source of supply in the early 1950s was the Philippines, which was joined by Malaysia around 1955-57. The two were joined by Indonesia after 1965. Exports of logs from the "big three" suppliers taken together thus increased at an astonishing pace

---

[1]Other major producing areas are Africa and Latin America.

4

throughout the postwar period; in the most recent period, 1965-70, they increased from 13 million $m^3(r)$ to 27.5 million $m^3(r)$, or at about 15 percent per annum. The three countries account for 97 percent of total log exports from the region, and indeed three-quarters of total log exports from all tropical regions including Africa and Latin America.

Japan has been the dominant importer of logs from the three Southeast Asian countries, accounting for roughly three-quarters of the latter's log exports. In the 1950s, as much as one-third of the logs imported by Japan were "re-exported" in the form of plywood, mainly to the U.S. market. Japan's plywood exports, consisting predominantly of tropical hardwood, grew rapidly in the 1950s but were basically unchanged through the 1960s. Most recently, they have been declining. Japan's imports of logs, however, have continued to rise rapidly due to expansion of domestic consumption. Consequently, the tropical hardwood content of Japan's plywood exports now is less than 5 percent of her annual intake of tropical hardwood.

Korea, Taiwan, and Singapore have also been significant and growing importers of logs from the Philippines, Malaysia, and Indonesia, and can be characterized as in-transit processor-exporters because they "re-export" most of the imported logs in the form of plywood, veneers, and sawnwood. Both Korea and Taiwan primarily export plywood, mainly to the U.S. market, while Singapore ships more than half of her exports in the form of sawnwood, and the rest in the form of plywood and veneers. Singapore's markets are well diversified.

Among the log-producing countries in this region, the Philippines is the only country that has a large plywood industry. Most of her plywood exports are destined to the United States. Her exports had grown steadily until they reached a peak level in 1968; they have since failed to expand further. Malaysia, mainly West Malaysia, also exports sizeable quantities of processed wood—in her case, primarily sawnwood. West Malaysia's sawnwood is shipped to such diversified markets as Europe, South Africa, Australia, Japan, and the United States. Indonesia exports very little processed wood.

Demand, Supply and Price Outlook for Tropical Hardwood in the Asia-Pacific Region

The dominant end markets for the Asia-Pacific region's tropical hardwood are Japan and the United States, and most of the tropical hardwood imported by these two countries in turn originates from the Asia-Pacific region. The estimated exportable volume of tropical hardwood of the Philippines, Malaysia, and Indonesia in 1975 and 1985 is compared with the projected imported demand by Japan and the United States for the corresponding years as follows:

	Million m³(r)	
	1975	1985
Export capacity of the Philippines, Malaysia, and Indonesia	40.7	43.0
Projected total import requirements of Japan and the United States	39.0	63.0
Potential import demand by Japan and the United States for the tropical hardwood produced by the Philippines, Malaysia, and Indonesia if the present relative shares of these suppliers in the Japanese and U.S. markets were maintained	36.0	52.2

In addition, the import demand by countries other than Japan and the United States for the tropical hardwood of the three major southeast Asian suppliers is likely to be about 4 million $m^3(r)$ in 1975 and substantially larger in 1985. It follows that, in 1975, the Philippine, Malaysian, and Indonesian volume of exportable tropical hardwood will just about meet the needs of their two largest, traditional "customers" as well as those of other minor (from the viewpoint of the Asian producers) "customers." It also follows that, by 1985, a large part of the increase in demand for tropical hardwood in Japan and the United States will have to be satisfied by trade flows from new sources, because of the limited export capacity of the traditional sources, even if demand by other importing countries does not increase materially between 1975 and 1985.

From the viewpoint of Japan and the United States, the most logical potential sources of additional tropical hardwood would be Papua/New Guinea and Latin America. However, there are two basic problems concerning the forest resources in these areas. One is that they contain a very low volume of timber per unit area, yielding only about one-third the volume per hectare found in a typical forest of the Philippines. Another problem is that both of these areas have forests of quite diverse species mixture. The processing, handling and marketing problems of such a varied mixture of species are much more difficult than those of the relatively uniform species mixture in the Philippines, Malaysia, and Indonesia. With the added problem of serious lack of infrastructural facilities, therefore, the per-unit cost of production of logs in these new areas is likely to be distinctly higher than that in the Philippines, Malaysia, and Indonesia. In the absence of any policy intervention on the part of the Philippines, Malaysia, and Indonesia, therefore, prices of tropical hardwood logs are likely to move up only slightly in the period to the mid-1970s but they are bound to rise sharply in the period beyond, barring drastic technological improvements in the production and transportation of tropical hardwood logs that would moderate the high costs of removing massive quantities of logs from forests in Papua/New Guinea and Latin America.

An important implication of the projected long-term rise in the prices of tropical hardwood logs would be that the timber resources in the Philippines, Malaysia, and Indonesia [Kalimantan] which are located in relatively more accessible areas, comparatively rich in per-hectare volume and relatively uniform in species mixture should command an increasing economic rent over time. In fact, the Philippines, Malaysia, and Indonesia combined have a virtual monopoly of relatively uniform (with respect to species), high density reserves of tropical hardwood. Since the price elasticity of demand for the combined log exports of the three countries does not seem to be high (as will be discussed later), *if* these three countries now *jointly* discourage the expansion of their exports of logs, they could earn more income per unit of logs exported in the immediate future, without jeopardizing the total foreign exchange earnings from log exports, while at the same time improving their future prospects for earning foreign exchanges from this source.

Wood Processing: An Ideal Vehicle of Industrial Growth in the Philippines, Malaysia, and Indonesia

As is often argued, if all logs that are currently exported in log form were locally processed and then exported in the form of sawnwood, veneer, and plywood, the foreign exchange earnings from forest products in the region could be at least two or three times what they are now.[2]

From the viewpoint of regional development strategy, primary processing of wood (production of sawnwood, veneers, and plywood) should take place largely in the Philippines, Malaysia, and Indonesia rather than in Japan, Korea, Taiwan, and Singapore. The wood processing industry is an ideal vehicle to accelerate an export-oriented industrial growth of the major log-producing countries at the present stage of their economic development.

Economic justification for encouraging the growth of primary wood processing industries in the log-producing, developing countries "at the expense of" the counterpart already established in another set of developing countries (Korea, Taiwan, and Singapore) rests mainly on the following four points.

---

[2]See for example Arnold [1] and Westoby [56].

i. Primary wood processing activities are typically weight- and volume-losing (hence freight-cost-saving) activities. Converting logs to sawnwood, plywood and veneers would lose 40 percent to 60 percent of the volume and weight of log raw material. Since ocean freight costs account for about one-fourth to one-third of average c.i.f. prices of tropical hardwood logs imported by Japan and Korea[3] and since the cost of log raw material accounts for as much as 65 percent to 80 percent of the total cost of producing sawnwood, veneers and plywood,[4] *ceteris paribus,* log-producing countries should have a considerable cost advantage in primary wood processing activities over log-importing processing countries.[5]

ii. Wood processing activities (excluding pulp and paper production[6] are relatively labor-intensive activities.[7] The Philippines, Malaysia, and Indonesia would have a comparative advantage in relatively labor-intensive activities rather than in capital-intensive activities at this stage of their development.

iii. Wood processing activities involve relatively simple technology and skill, while requiring relatively small investments in establishing factories of economic size. The Philippines, Malaysia, and Indonesia should start with relatively simple products while Korea, Taiwan, and Singapore should specialize in more advanced products, such as plywoods with chemical finish, various overlays, and printed face, and in secondary processing, for example furniture components, window frames, and door skins.

iv. Wood processing activities could serve as a starter of the industrialization process in the "remote areas" (outer islands) — Mindanao, Sabah, Sarawak, and Kalimantan — where most of the logs that are currently exported are being produced.

---

[3]For example, the unit value of lauan and apitong logs imported by Japan (c.i.f. Japanese ports) from all sources are about U.S.$30-$31 per m^3 and the estimated average cost of transporting logs from the exporting countries (Philippines, Sabah, Sarawak, Indonesia, and others) is about $8-$10 per m^3.

[4]Based on Chusho Kigyo Shinko Jigyodan [5]. The share of logs in total cost has come down recently.

[5]There are two factors which tend to "weaken" the argument: it is more expensive to transport plywood and other processed wood products because these products require special packing; and the wood residues resulting from sawmilling and plywood manufacturing are often utilized for chipboard and pulp. These considerations, however, do not change the basic argument.

[6] *Wood processing* here excludes pulp and paper production unless otherwise noted.

[7]See Snape [45]. By using Hal B. Lary's method, Snape shows that sawmilling, plywood, and veneer production are relatively labor intensive in the United States and Australia. He contends that, since factor intensity reversals seldom occur in reality, timber processing may be considered a labor intensive activity in all the relevant countries.

Problems in the Growth of Processed Wood Exports from the Log-Producing Countries

Evidence abounds that it has been far more profitable for the timber companies operating in the Philippines, Malaysia, and Indonesia to export logs rather than to process the wood first and then export it in processed forms. Specific reasons for the failure of the log-producing countries to accelerate the exports of processed wood include: the tariff escalation (high tariff on processed products, low or no tariffs on unprocessed products) in the developed importing countries; the lack of opportunities in the log-producing countries to utilize wood residues economically, which would in effect reduce the cost of production of sawnwood, veneers, and plywood; the difficulties which the wood processing firms in the log-producing countries have been experiencing in obtaining necessary supplies of equipment, parts, and such essential inputs as resins (glues) for plywood production at reasonable costs; the generally low levels of technical skills of available labor in the log-producing countries; and the poor infrastructure in the log-producing countries, especially with respect to internal transportation.[8]

Broadly speaking, tropical hardwood trade in the Asia-Pacific region involves three types of trading parties, that is, the developed importer-consumer countries (Japan, the United States, and others), the developing "in-transit" processor countries (Korea, Taiwan, and Singapore) and the log-producing developing countries (the Philippines, Malaysia, and Indonesia). These three groups of countries have had generally different types of industrial and trade policies. First is the basically "inward-looking" industrial policies of the Philippines and Indonesia; they have not helped the growth of exports of processed wood products, but have ac-

---

[8]Timber processing industries in the Philippines, Malaysia, and Indonesia are handicapped by costly transportation and shipping, either local or international or both. In the Philippines the bulk of timber processing capacity is scattered throughout the island of Mindanao, and in the Cagayan Valley region of Luzon island. Because shipping points are scattered, the per unit cost of export freight tends to be high. As long as the present pattern of plant location and internal transportation system including handling and storage at ports does not improve, the Philippine wood industries will continue to be handicapped in exporting processed products in the international market (see Sycip, Gorres, Velayo & Co. [47], pp. 199-174). In Indonesia, again, there is a very major problem of an inefficient and unreliable internal transportation system. A major portion of log raw material production occurs in Kalimantan but there is very little infrastructure support, at the moment, to establish the timber processing industry there. Yet, the growth of the Kalimantan log-based timber processing industry in Java, where there is better infrastructure, is hindered principally by the poor and costly interisland transport system. It is imperative, therefore, that the infrastructure in Kalimantan and the interisland transportation be improved in order for Indonesia to be able to establish a competitive timber processing industry.

tually tended to penalize the exports of processed wood products.[9] Second is the decisively "outward-looking" industrial policies of Korea and Taiwan (since the mid-1960s) and Singapore (since independence); these have favored the growth of export-oriented manufacturing activities including plywood manufacturing based on imported logs.[10] Third is the protectionistic trade policies of developed importing countries, especially Japan and the United States, with respect to most "light manufacturing" activities, including wood processing industries; the policies have been reflected in the "tariff escalation" of these countries.[11]

It is the combination of these different types of industrial and trade policies of the major parties involved that has strongly conditioned the pattern of tropical hardwood trade in the Asia-Pacific region. Taking into account the most rational evolution of production and trade patterns in tropical hardwood, it would be to the mutual advantage of these three parties to adjust their industrial and trade policies to encourage and accelerate the probable long-term developments.

A Strategy for Accelerating the Growth of
Processed Wood Exports from the Log-Producing Countries

In recent years the Philippines and Indonesia have changed their industrial and trade policies from being markedly inward-looking to generally outward-looking. To assure a decisive success in their processed wood exports, their outward-looking policies will probably have to be developed even further. Partly due to the early and decisive change of policy in this regard, West Malaysia is now exporting two-thirds of its wood in processed form, mainly sawnwood.

With respect to policies more specifically related to wood processing, the three major log-exporting countries could encourage wood processing at home by: discouraging the export of logs by jointly maintaining substantial export taxes; encouraging the growth of export-oriented wood

---

[9]The inward-looking trade policies of the past, especially in the Philippines and Indonesia, although changing gradually to outward-looking, have resulted in considerable difficulties for wood processing companies—difficulties in obtaining necessary equipment, machinery parts, and essential nonwood inputs such as resin (needed for plywood) at competitive cost due to exchange controls and overvaluation of currencies. Referring to the case of the Philippines, John H. Power and Gerardo P. Sicat go so far as to state: "... while a host of reasons have been set forth in attempts to explain why the Philippines exports logs to Korea and Taiwan where they are made into plywood for re-export, a sufficient explanation appears to be the protection system and the unfavorable exchange rate which it defends. This suggests that many other potential export industries based on domestic raw materials may also be victims of the protection system." Power and Sicat [39], p. 107.
[10]Balassa [2].
[11]Balassa [3], pp. 194-195; see also Annex V.

10

processing industries by providing comprehensive "packages" of incentives; adjusting their forestry concession policies so as to discourage exports of logs and encourage exports of processed products; and improving infrastructure to induce rapid growth of export-oriented wood processing industries.[12]

In implementing these policies, it is helpful to have a vision of an ideal form of the industry's organization. A recent report prepared for the FAO by the Tuolumne Corporation recommends that "the best solution to overcoming the obstructive conservatism of the industry in fulfilling the market function is industry reform with vertical integration from the markets on down."[13] Such integration can take a number of forms. A single company could handle all steps from the resource through processing, shipping, distribution, and even application in end use. Or an integration could be effectively achieved by contractual arrangements, partial integration, and joint ventures. The ideal industrial structure is further visualized as one that has deep penetration in a variety of market sectors, is not concentrated enough to exercise monopoly control of the resource and processing industry, and has a vested interest in maximizing processing and species utilization.

Joint discouragement of log exports would be of mutual benefit to the three log-exporting countries. For instance, if the Philippines and Malaysia alone would restrict log exports but Indonesia would not, then Indonesian logs would fill most, if not all, of trade volume now moving in log form. The result would be that the newly developing wood processing industries in the Philippines and Malaysia would suffer in competing with the established industries of the traditional log-importing countries. Regional cooperation is clearly in the long-term interests of the countries involved.

One question often raised in connection with this type of action is: would the exporters of the commodity in question (in this case, logs) not lose in terms of total foreign exchange earnings from that commodity because, although they will get a higher average price per unit of the commodity exported than otherwise, they will be selling less volume than otherwise?[14] They would not lose in total foreign exchange earnings, if the price elasticity of demand facing the suppliers acting jointly happens to be equal to or less than unity. On the other hand, they *would* lose in total exchange earnings if the elasticity happens to be greater than unity.

Unfortunately, no reliable estimate of the price elasticity of demand for the log exports of these countries is available. However, there are some

---

[12]Among others, see Turbang and von Hegel [50], especially pp. 516-518.

[13]The Tuolumne Corporation [49], p. 16.

[14]See interesting discussions on this point in Manning [34] and Garnaut [22].

11

circumstantial reasons to believe that the demand is not very elastic within the relevant price range. Demand for tropical hardwood in general is price inelastic because the demand for processed products made from tropical hardwood is generally inelastic. Domestic supply of the closest substitute, temperate hardwood, in the importing countries is quite inelastic. Softwoods and nonwood materials are good substitutes for the logs coming from the "big three" suppliers only in limited end uses. The cost of getting tropical hardwood logs in great quantities from alternative sources such as Indochina, the southwest Pacific islands, and Latin America would be much higher than the existing conditions because of political insecurities (Indochina), higher freight costs (Latin America), and generally higher cost of production due to lower incidence of merchantable volume per hectare (in all of the alternative source areas). Logs from the possible alternative sources are inferior substitutes because of their diversity of species mixture and smaller average sizes.

One countervailing factor that would tend to make the demand less inelastic is the exports to distant markets such as Europe. Currently, in competition with tropical hardwood coming from Africa, some logs are being exported to European markets from the three Southeast-Asian countries. If the prices of the logs coming from the latter are raised and the prices of those from Africa are not, the log exports from the Asian countries could be reduced or even eliminated. However, since the volume of log exports to Europe is relatively small compared with the total log exports from the "big three" Asian exporters, the effect of loss in the European market would be marginal.

The price elasticity of demand for log exports of the three major Asian exporters is probably less than unity or, at worst, not much larger than unity except in high price range. By acting jointly to discourage log exports, the Philippines, Malaysia, and Indonesia would not lose much, if at all, in terms of their total foreign exchange earnings from logs, while they will have much to gain if the measure contributes toward accelerating their exports of processed products.

It cannot be overemphasized that, despite many possible difficulties, it would be advantageous for the Philippines, Malaysia, and Indonesia to cooperate closely in implementing the general policies mentioned above. It is obvious that the levels of export taxes must be set through close consultations among these three countries. It is equally important that the national policies of export incentives for processed products and forestry concessions be internationally coordinated. The three countries can also benefit from consultations on the matter of infrastructure, since this involves shipping and stocking. Already, some international cooperation exists among the log-producing countries, and some small initial steps have been taken. In 1969, the Philippines and Indonesia concluded eight agreements on economic and technical cooperation, two of which bear directly upon forestry and forest industries. Although the first meeting of the Joint Philippine-Indonesian Commission on Economic and Technical Cooperation was held only as late as in July 1971, the spirit of cooperation is evidently being enhanced.[15] Similarly, through the Association of Southeast Asian Nations (ASEAN), membership in which includes Indonesia, Malaysia, the Philippines, as well as Singapore and Thailand, economic and trade cooperation on timber processing, among others, is being studied.

It would be in the interest of the United States, Japan, and other importers of tropical hardwood, as well as in the interest of the lesser developed countries, if these developed nations adjusted their policies to anticipate the long-term trends in development of the industry and to facilitate the adjustments needed. An effective means of such an adjustment would be a significant reduction (and eventual elimination) of import duties on the processed tropical hardwood coming from lesser developed countries. Under the UNCTAD Generalized Preference Scheme, many developed countries made offers of duty-free access for manufactures and semimanufactures originating in developing countries, including processed wood products, but they are all subject to safeguard mechanisms, either tariff quotas or escape clauses. Japan's offer, which was implemented on August 1, 1971, included only a 50 percent reduction of duties on sawnwood and veneers, and no reduction on plywood. The American offer has not yet been ratified by the U.S. Congress. It is desirable that further positive steps soon be taken by all developed countries to reduce the import barriers against tropical hardwood products coming from LDC exporters. (See Annex 2.)

In the meantime, Japanese plywood manufacturers should probably specialize in sophisticated products, for example, plywoods with printed face, chemical and other special finishes and various overlays, and products of exceptionally high standards of fire-resistance.[16] They may aim at diversifying themselves vertically, for instance, into the prefabricated housing industry. They should also be encouraged to participate in joint

---

[15]For specific results of the progress, see Paterno [37].

[16]It is impractical to say that further steps toward total elimination of import barriers in developing countries against imports of processed tropical hardwood from developing exporters should be taken without parallel steps to abet the survival of existing enterprises in wood processing industries in the developed countries attempting to restructure themselves. The Japanese government has been taking steps to transform the plywood industries under the Small and Medium Business Modernization Act of 1969. See Japan, Forestry Agency [27], pp. 65-69.

ventures in plywood manufacturing in the log-producing countries and import plain plywood for further processing in Japan.

Finally, the in-transit processor countries—principally Korea, Taiwan, and Singapore—should gradually grow out of the reliance on the export of plain primary processed products. In the cases of Korea and Taiwan, plywood exports are contributing very little in the way of foreign exchange earnings as a result of excessively generous incentives for export. It is reported that, in Korea, there was on average a net loss of 28¢ to 29¢ per U.S. dollar earned by exporting plywood in 1967-69.[17] In Singapore, in spite of rapid progress in recent years and the excellent growth prospects in the immediate future, the timber processing industry envisages some serious problems in the longer term. Major problems other than the prospective log supply are the increasing scarcity of land space and the possible labor shortage and rising labor costs. Singapore is a very small island country whose economy is growing very rapidly, at the rate of well over 10 percent per annum. The opportunity cost of land space is rapidly rising. Similarly, as a result of the rapid economic growth, the labor market is already quite tight and labor costs are going up rapidly. In fact, many of the timber processing factories today employ a large number of Malaysian nationals on temporary work permits.

Thus, it seems to be in the long-run interest of the in-transit processor countries to move toward specialization in the exports of wood products involving a "higher degree of processing," higher value added, and larger net foreign exchange earnings. These countries would be better off if they moved increasingly into so-called secondary processing, that is, prefinished plywood, furniture components, and so forth.

Need for Better Control of Timber Resources: A Long-Term Forestry Policy

As mentioned earlier, world demand for tropical hardwood is expected to continue its rapid growth for at least another decade and, quite possibly, much longer. In the meantime, as a result of the rapid growth of export demand for timber, some of the traditional sources of supply in the region, such as the Philippines and West Malaysia, are being threatened with possible depletion of timber resources in the near future. The experience of the Philippines and, to some extent, that of Sabah and Sarawak, indicates a wasteful use of timber resources due to poor and shortsighted logging practices and a lack of adequate forest management. Indonesia, at the moment, boasts "unlimited" forest resources, but will have to face the problem of depletion eventually and would be well advised to take appropriate measures to avoid wasteful use of its resources as soon as possible, and to maximize the long-run benefits for the nation's economy.

---

[17]Korea Productivity Center [33], pp. 124-126.

One possibility to alleviate the depletion threats in the forest resources of the Philippines, Malaysia, and Indonesia is fast-growing forest plantations. Man-made forests are growing in importance as sources of industrial wood around the world. Demand for paper and hence for wood material for paper-making is growing fast in the developing countries as well as in the rest of the world. It is highly desirable for developing countries to be able to meet their growing paper needs themselves at competitive costs. Although the hardwoods they do possess in natural forests are increasingly used for pulping, at present the bulk of the grades supplied through the trade are made from long-fiber softwoods. Long-fiber softwoods occur indigenously only in limited quantities and limited areas in the tropical countries. But there are vast areas in the Southeast Asian countries where exotic softwoods and pulpable hardwoods could be grown in man-made forests. The possibilities of forest plantations using a few fast-growing species in the Philippines, Malaysia, and Indonesia should be studied. These plantations could provide additional low-cost wood material for pulp and paper and other forest industries in the three countries in the longer run.

Policy Implications

The findings of this paper have several implications for the countries involved:

i. It would be advantageous for the Philippines, Malaysia, and Indonesia to coordinate their timber policies.

ii. It would be in the long-run interest of Korea, Taiwan, and Singapore to "up-grade" their wood industries to produce increasingly more sophisticated wood products.

iii. In order to facilitate these changes and anticipate long-term trends, the major developed countries which import tropical timber (mainly Japan and the United States) should reduce their tariff barriers to imports of processed wood products coming from developing countries.

iv. International financial institutions should probably follow a more active investment policy to foster these changes in the developing countries in the Asia-Pacific region. Investment opportunities can be found in infrastructure (internal land and sea transportation and public utilities),[18] primary wood processing industries (mainly in the log-producing countries), secondary wood processing industries

---

[18]Since the forest areas in these countries are in remote, principally jungle regions, public utilities, schools, port facilities, highways, railroads, water supply systems, and so forth are needed. Investment possibilities are vast.

(mainly in the in-transit processor countries), fast-growing forestry plantations, pulp and paper projects, and forestry education.

v. The efforts of UNDP, UNCTAD, and FAO toward an early establishment of the proposed Tropical Timber Bureau should be supported. The Bureau could provide effective global machinery to promote tropical hardwood exports of developing countries, including those in the Asia-Pacific region, if it is conceived and organized properly. (See Annex 3.)

Furthermore, possible investment strategies on the part of international financial institutions aimed at opening up currently "inaccessible" tropical hardwood resources in Latin America and remote areas of Africa should be studied by these institutions, in view of the expected rising world prices of tropical hardwoods. Opening up new areas will restrain soaring prices but, since the costs of opening up these areas would be high, prices would likely stabilize at relatively high levels. The three Asian countries where costs of exploitation are much lower should be able to soak up a large part of the producers' surplus, if government policies and institutional arrangements are conducive.

II. Trends in World Wood Economy

The purpose of this chapter is to examine general trends in world production, consumption, and trade of all forest products, softwood as well as hardwood, to provide a proper perspective for understanding the problems and prospects of tropical hardwood.

Trends in the Production and
Consumption of Forest Products

Forest products are classified, in terms of broad uses, into fuelwood and industrial wood. The latter, in turn, may be classified into three broad categories—logs,[1] pulpwood, and other industrial wood.[2] Table 2.1 shows the world's recorded production[3] (consumption[4]) of forest products in selected years. World recorded production of wood in 1969 was about 2.14 billion $m^3(r)$, of which 56 percent was industrial wood and the balance fuelwood.[5] About 60 percent of the industrial wood is logs, about 25 percent pulpwood,[6] and the remainder "other industrial wood."

---

[1]Includes sawlogs, veneer logs, and logs for sleepers.

[2]Includes poles, posts, pilings, and so forth.

[3]Because of the existence of unrecorded production in all categories, the "recorded" statistics tend to underestimate actual production. Unrecorded production is quite small in the case of logs and pulpwood (not more than 0.5 percent of the recorded), but is probably substantial in the case of other industrial wood and fuelwood (over 10 percent of the recorded).

[4]World consumption is assumed to be equal to world production.

[5]Statistics on fuelwood are poor. Since very little goes into trade, fuelwood will generally be ignored in this paper.

[6]FAO statistics do not separate pulpwood from pitprops (mine timber) for early years. Currently, world production of pitprops amounted to about 39 million $m^3(r)$ in 1969 and accounted for 12 percent of the total pulpwood and pitprops produced in that year. Consumption of pitprops is expected to decline in the future.

Table 2.1: Change in Recorded World Use of Wood and Wood Products, 1950-52 to 1969

| | millions units | 1951[1] | 1956[1] | 1961[1] | 1968 | 1969 | Change 1951-69 | | |
							volume	index 1951=100	1961-69 %/year
WOOD IN UNPROCESSED FORM									
Logs[2]	m³(r)	493.4	582.2	648.3	727.3	735.2	241.8	149	1.6
Pulpwood[3] & pitprops	" "	185.6	233.5	255.6	301.8	315.8	130.2	170	2.7
Other industrial wood[4]	" "	129.2	124.9	116.3	161.5	160.8	31.6	124	4.1
Total industrial wood	" "	808.2	940.6	1,020.2	1,190.6	1,211.8	403.6	150	2.2
Fuelwood	" "	865.6	876.1	876.5	919.2	932.9	67.3	108	0.8
Total Wood	" "	1,673.8	1,816.7	1,896.7	2,109.8	2,144.8	471.0	128	1.5
WOOD PRODUCTS									
Sawnwood[5]	m³(s)	266.1	309.6	341.0	401.0	408.5	—	154	2.3
Paper and paperboard	metric tons	44.3	59.4	77.3	114.3	122.6	—	277	5.9
Plywood	m³(s)	6.8	11.3	16.8	30.0	30.7	—	451	7.8
Fiberboard	metric tons	2.2	3.3	4.5	7.2	7.5	—	341	6.6
Particle board	" "	0.04	0.57	2.29	13.69	16.09	—	40,225	28.0
Miscellaneous Roundwood[6]	m³(r)	129.2	124.9	116.3	161.5	160.8	—	124	4.1

[1]Three year averages of 1950-52, 1955-57, and so on
[2]Sawlogs, veneer logs, and logs for sleepers
[3]Includes roundwood used for the manufacture of particle board and fiberboard
[4]FAO statistics show a sharp increase from 115.6 in 1964 to 150.7 in 1965, mainly due to a sudden increase in the USSR from 53.9 in 1964 to 87.8 in 1965, apparently because of a change in coverage
[5]Includes sleepers
[6]Excludes pitprops

Source: FAO [21], p. 51 and [20; 1969-70 ed.], pp. 18-47.

18

The most important categories of wood in unprocessed form are logs and pulpwood. As can be seen from Table 2.1, the largest *increase in absolute volume* between 1951 and 1969 occurred in the log category. Logs accounted for 60 percent of the total increase in the production of industrial wood. The highest *rate of growth,* however, was experienced by the pulpwood category during this period. The relatively significant increase in other industrial wood as observed from the recorded statistics is more apparent than real.[7] The actual trend in this category is believed to have been rather static for the last two decades and world demand for this category of industrial wood is expected to decrease slowly by 1985.

The most important trend in the world wood economy in the last two decades from the viewpoint of developing countries has been the growing importance of tropical hardwood in world production and consumption of logs. Table 2.2 shows world production (consumption) of logs by broad specie groups in 1954-56, 1964-66, and 1968. From the mid-1950s to 1968, annual production of logs increased by 147 million $m^3(r)$, or by 25.5 percent. Conifers or softwood, more than 85 percent of which is produced in developed countries and centrally planned economy countries (CPEs), accounted for 70 percent of this increase in absolute volume. Hardwood accounted for 30 percent. In terms of percentage increases, however, tropical hardwood, which is produced entirely in developing countries, increased several times more rapidly than softwood. Temperate hardwood hardly had any growth at all—less than one percent a year. This trend for greater importance of tropical hardwood in world production of logs is expected to continue.

Turning to trends in *processed wood products,* one finds that the growth in *sawnwood* has been the slowest among the major product groups represented in Table 2.1. The slow growth in sawnwood is responsible for the slow growth in the log production. However, it must be noted that hardwood sawnwood has expanded faster than softwood sawnwood in recent years, as evidenced by the figures below:

	1961-63 average	1969	Index
	million $m^3(r)$		1961-63=100
Sawnwood			
softwood	267.2	306.8	115
hardwood	74.0	93.0	126

Source: FAO [20; 1961, 1962, 1963, and 1969-70 eds.].

---

[7]Table 2.1, n. 4.

19

Table 2.2 : World Production (Consumption) of Logs[1] by Specie Groups, 1954-56, 1964-66, and 1968

(million m³(r) per annum)

| Specie Group | Three-year averages | | | Increase from 1954-56 to 1968 | |
	1954-56	1964-66	1968	in absolute volume	in percentage
All logs	577.6	689.4	725.0	147.4	25.5
Softwood logs	431.2	509.4	531.7	100.5	23.3
Hardwood logs	146.4	180.0	193.3	46.9	32.0
Tropical hardwood	38.6	58.3	71.2	32.6	84.4
Temperate hardwood	107.8	121.7	122.1	14.3	13.2

[1]Logs include sawlogs, veneer logs, and logs for sleepers
Source: FAO [20; 1954-68 eds.] and [18].

The rate of growth in sawnwood has been slow partly due to substitution by other wood and nonwood materials. Among the products substituting for sawnwood, especially in developed countries, are *wood-based panel products*—plywood, particle board, fiberboard, and so forth,[8] which have demonstrated high rates of growth in the last two decades (Table 2.1). Substitution has been encouraged by two factors: a declining trend of prices of wood-based panel products *relative* to those of sawnwood, and the relative ease with which panel products can be installed. In addition to substituting for sawnwood, panel products have found new applications. FAO projections indicate that world consumption of wood-based panels is likely to rise rapidly from 31.8 million metric tons per annum in 1966-68 to 74.7 million metric tons by 1980, or at an annual rate of 6.4 percent.[9] Unfortunately, no statistics are available to indicate the relative proportions of softwood and hardwood used in the production of various wood-based panel products on a worldwide basis. In the case of plywood, it is estimated that, as of 1963-65, softwood plywood and hardwood plywood accounted for 56 percent and 44 percent of world production respectively.[10] More than half of raw materials used for production of fiberboard and particle board is industrial wood residues and nonwood materials such as bagasse; only less than half is roundwood.

Another fast-growing product group has been *paper and paperboard*. Per capita consumption of paper and paperboard is highly correlated with per capita income. The relation, however, is not a linear one. In fact, income

---

[8]Veneers are normally included in wood-based panel products. Veneers, however, are used mostly for making plywood and as surfacing material for other wood products such as blockboard, particle board, and fiberboard.
[9]FAO Committee on Wood-Based Panel Products [19].
[10]Singh [44], Table 1.

20

elasticity declines as income rises.[11] According to FAO projections,[12] demand for paper and paperboard is estimated to grow at 5.3 percent per annum between 1968 and 1985 — a rate slower than the average rate in the past of 5.9 percent per annum but still a respectable rate of growth. The fast growth in paper and paperboard and the fast growth in particle board and fiberboard have been responsible for the rather high rate of growth in the demand for pulpwood.

The fiber raw materials for paper making can be divided into three main categories (percentage proportions in 1963 provided in parentheses): wood pulp (77 percent), nonwood pulp (5 percent) and waste paper (18 percent).[13] The pattern of raw material supplies available for, and utilized by, the pulp and paper industry has been changing. The most important developments have been the rapidly expanding use of wood residues, the growing use of hardwood, the rapid growth of pulp and paper production based on fast-growing plantation species, and the declining impor-

Table 2.3: World Requirements (in Roundwood Equivalent) of Wood and Wood Products, 1962, and Projections to 1975, 1980, and 1985

	1962[1] m³(r)	1975 m³(r)	1980 m³(r)[2]	1985 m³(r)[2]
Sawnwood[3]	590.0	723.7	775.1	829.3
Panels[4]	65.5	152.7	200.0	(255.3)
Paper & Paperboard[5]	217.5	441.8	572.2	742.4
Other Industrial Roundwood[6, 7]	176	170	(169)	168
Total Industrial Wood[6, 7]	1,049	1,488	1,716	1,995
Fuelwood[7]	1,017	1,036	(1,049)	1,064
Total	2,066	2,524	2,765	3,059

[1]Three-year averages of 1961-63
[2]Figures in parentheses are estimates made by the author
[3]Based on the conversion factors recommended in FAO [20; 1969 ed.]
[4]1962, 1975, and 1980—estimates based on the conversion factors in FAO [20]. The wood requirements thus estimated tend to overestimate the roundwood required for the wood-based panel products to the extent that the products are produced from wastes and residues. The estimate for 1985 is based on the assumption that the total wood requirement for wood-based panels would increase at 5 percent a year during 1980-1985
[5]A conversion factor of 2.7324 m³(r) per metric ton of paper and paperboard was used. This was inferred from the data in Tables 3 and 5 in FAO [11], I, pp. 322, 336
[6]Includes pitprops
[7]Estimated total consumption, which differs from recorded consumption shown in FAO [20] by an allowance for unrecorded consumption
Source: FAO [14], I and [12].

---

[11]For FAO's basic work in this field, see [17].
[12]FAO [14].
[13]FAO [21], p. 81.

tance of nonwood pulp and waste paper as fiber raw materials for paper making.[14]

Demand Prospects for Wood

Projected world requirements of wood and wood products are shown in Table 2.3, in terms of roundwood equivalent, for 1975, 1980, and 1985. According to the projections which are only intended to indicate broad ofders of magnitude, the world's requirements of industrial wood are to grow at the average rate of 2.7 percent per annum between 1962 and 1975, and at 3 percent per annum during the 1975-1985 period, to reach almost two billion cubic meters per year by 1985.

The projected requirements of wood in roundwood equivalents are associated with the projected growth rates in requirements of major wood and wood products given below:

	Projected Growth Rates for Major Wood Products (in percents per annum)	
	1967-1975	**1975-1985**
Sawnwood	1.4	1.4
Wood-based panels	7.3	5.5
Paper and paperboard	5.2	8.3

Source: Based on Table 2.4.

Trends in World Trade in Forest Products

In the nine-year period from 1960 to 1969, world exports of *all forest products*[15] increased from U.S.$6.2 billion to U.S.$12.7 billion—at an average rate of 8.3 percent per annum—in keeping pace with the growth of total world trade in all commodities including manufactures.[16] An important trend in the trade of forest products in the last decade or so has been the rapid rise in exports from developing countries. Forest product exports of these countries increased from U.S.$515 million in 1960 to U.S.$1.66 billion in 1969. The growth has been much faster than that of total world trade of forest products.

[14]These projections, which are based on research undertaken in the mid-1960s (FAO [21], pp. 81-85), may prove to be somewhat on the low side in view of the record in the last few years. The demand projections for the United States, Japan, and Europe presented in Chapter IV, however, take account of the latest projections made by respective authoritative sources. Therefore, the projections presented in this section are not consistent with those for the above-mentioned regions as presented in Chapter IV. Demand projections for tropical hardwood as presented in Chapter IV, however, do not depend on the demand projections for all species as presented in this section.

[15]Including such "miscellaneous minor items" as fuelwood, charcoal, poles, wood residues, chips and particles, raw cork and cork manufactures, waste paper and nonwood pulp and paper articles.

[16]Analysis in this section owes a great deal to FAO [20; 1969-70 ed.], pp. x-xvi and [13], pp. 609-650.

Table 2.4: World Consumption of Selected Forest Products—Past Trends (1954-68) and Projections (1975, 1980, 1985)

	Unit	Actual[1]					Projected[2]			Per Annum Growth Rate (percent)			
		1954-56 Average	1961-63 Average	1964-66 Average	1966-68 Average	1968	1975	1980	1985	1961-63 to 1966-68	1966-68 to 1975	1975 to 1980	1975 to 1985
Sawnwood	million m³(s)	298.8	341.2	372.1	379.9	388.9	423.8	453.4	484.5	2.0	1.4	—	1.4
softwood	" " "	—	267.2	288.0	292.9	301.3	317.6	333.8	349.7	—	—	—	—
hardwood	" " "	—	74.0	84.1	87.0	87.6	106.2	119.6	134.8	—	—	—	—
Wood-based Panels													
plywood and veneer	million m tons	n.a.	22.0	27.2	31.8	n.a.	55.8	74.7	n.a.	7.6	7.3	6.0	—
fiberboard and particle board	million m³	n.a.	21.7	24.7	27.8	n.a.	43.0	53.5	n.a.	5.1	5.6	4.5	—
particle board	million m tons	3.4	7.8	10.8	13.5	15.6	26.9	38.5	n.a.	11.6	9.0	7.5	—
fiberboard	million m tons	3.1	5.0	5.6	6.6	7.05	10.3	13.3	n.a.	5.7	5.7	5.3	—
particle board	million m tons	0.3	2.8	5.2	6.9	8.58	17.1	26.5	n.a.	20.0	12.0	9.2	—
Paper and Paperboard	million m tons	56.1	79.6	98.0	107.9	112.3	161.7	209.4	271.7	6.3	5.2	—	5.3

[1] Data for "plywood and veneer" and "Wood-based Panels (aggregate)"—1961-63 from FAO [14]; 1964-66 and 1966-68 from FAO [12]
Historical data for all other items based on *Yearbook*

[2] All projections for wood-based panel products for 1975 and 1980 are based on FAO [12]. All other projections for 1975 and all projections for 1985 are based on FAO [14]. Projections for sawnwood and paper and paperboard for 1980 are Bank staff estimates made by interpolation

Source: FAO [12], [14], [20].

Despite the above tendency, however, it is still the exports of developed countries that dominate the scene. In 1969, these countries exported forest products (including all miscellaneous items) worth U.S.$9.96 billion accounting for 77 percent of total world exports.

Developing countries tend to export products with little or no degree of processing and import wood with a high degree of processing. As can be seen from Table 2.5, in 1968 more than half of developing countries' export earnings from forest products stemmed from unprocessed roundwood. Sawnwood accounted for about one-quarter, wood-based panels about one-fifth. Pulp and paper exports of developing countries were negligible. On the import side, over 60 percent of the forest product imports of developing countries was accounted for by pulp and paper. The heavy burden of pulp and paper imports is evidenced by the fact that more than half of the export earnings from all forest products is offset by the paper and paperboard imports alone, and the need for the latter is expected to continue to grow rapidly.

Growth of trade in logs, both softwood and hardwood, has been spectacular. World exports of *softwood logs,* consisting mainly of the flow from North America and the USSR to Japan, surged from 1.85 million $m^3(r)$ in 1955 to 24.3 million $m^3(r)$ in 1970. In the latter year, 70 percent of the volume was imported by Japan.

Similarly, world exports of *hardwood logs* increased at an astonishing pace, from about 7 million $m^3(r)$ in 1955 to 29 million $m^3(r)$ in 1968, and to preliminary estimates of 34 and 39 million $m^3(r)$ in 1969 and 1970 respectively.[17] A substantial part of this massive trade consists of logs from Southeast Asia to Japan, but also to Taiwan and the Republic of Korea. Another important trade flow of hardwood logs consists of exports from West and West Central Africa to Western Europe.

Although the growth of world trade in *pulpwood* in the round or split form has been rather modest (increasing from 12.9 million $m^3(r)$ in 1955 to 18.9 million $m^3(r)$ in 1970), a new feature has been the emergence of the trade in *woodchips* which are used for pulping. World trade in this commodity is confined mainly to exports from developed countries to developed countries, the main flows being from North America and Oceania to Japan. Tropical species are not yet involved in this trade in any significant way, but active investigations into possible chipping projects in tropical forests are under way.

Trade in *sawnwood,* which is dominated by softwood, has been expanding only very slowly, from 35.8 million $m^3(s)$ in 1955 to 55.4 million $m^3(s)$ in 1970. In 1970, *softwood* accounted for 87 percent of world exports of sawnwood. Main flows in softwood sawnwood are from the northern part

---

[17]FAO [20; 1969-70 ed.], p. 49 and [13], p. 206.

24

Table 2.5: Trade of Major Forest Products in 1968 World and Economic Classes

(million U.S.$[1])

Product group	World		Developed market economy countries		Developing countries		Centrally planned countries	
	Exports	Imports	Exports	Imports	Exports	Imports	Exports	Imports
Roundwood	1,445	2,056	511	1,748	677	196	257	112
Sawnwood	2,251	2,580	1,511	2,203	279	224	461	153
Wood-based panels	930	964	630	849	221	68	79	47
Wood pulp	1,825	1,959	1,728	1,671	33	155	64	133
Paper and board	3,391	3,645	3,225	2,698	44	690	122	257
All products	9,842	11,204	7,605	9,169	1,254	1,333	983	702

[1]Exports in f.o.b. values, imports in c.i.f. values

Source: FAO [20; 1969-70 ed.], p. xii.

25

of Europe to the rest of Europe, from Canada to the United States, and from the USSR to Europe. Trade in *hardwood* sawnwood is very fragmented.

Wood-based panel products have been the most dramatic of all forest products in the expansion of exports since 1960. Although in 1960 about two-thirds of *plywood* exports originated in developed countries and only 13 percent in the developing countries, by 1970 the latter countries' share in world exports had increased to over 40 percent. Korea and Taiwan with very limited forest resources have been the most successful examples of the growing plywood export trade from the developing countries. *Veneer sheets* also provide another successful example of fast-growing forest product trade from developing countries. *Particle board* trade tends to be relatively small and localized because of its low value per unit weight. Trade in *fiberboard* is also minor.

Production of *pulp and paper* has traditionally been based on the use of softwood resources. Thus Canada, the United States, and the Nordic countries have dominated the export trade in this sector. It is a capital-intensive industry requiring a higher degree of technical know-how as compared with other forest industries. Production, consumption and trade of pulp and paper take place mostly among developed countries.

III. Sources of Tropical Hardwood

Table 3.1 indicates area estimates of hardwood forests in the world, which is divided into eight regions, in comparison with those of all forests. In South America, Africa, Asia, and the Pacific,[1] hardwood (broad-leaved) forests make up from 82 percent to 99 percent of the region's total forest area. In Central America, the proportion of hardwood forests (51 percent) is smaller than those in the four regions mentioned above, but still is substantially higher than those in Europe, the USSR, North America, and so forth. South America, Africa, and Asia, which contain most of the tropical forests in the world in addition to some temperate forests, account for 75 percent of the world's *hardwood* forests although the three regions account for only 53 percent of all the world's forests.

Table 3.1 also shows FAO's rough estimates of the growing stock of hardwood forests in various regions. According to these estimates, South America alone has 57 percent of the total volume of hardwood stock and Asia and Africa together have 24 percent of the total. In other words, the three regions which account for most of tropical forests contain over 80 percent of the world's standing volume of hardwood species. Geographically, tropical hardwood producing countries are grouped into three regions: tropical Africa (Africa excluding North African countries and the Republic of South Africa), tropical Latin America (Central and South America excluding Argentina, Chile, and Uruguay), and tropical Asia-Pacific (Southeast Asia, South Asia, and southwest Pacific islands).

[1]The "Pacific" in this paragraph includes all of Oceania including New Zealand and Australia.

Table 3.1 World's Hardwood Forest Resources

Region	Total land area million ha.	Area of all forests million ha.	Area of hardwood forests		Relation of hardwood forest to all forest in region Percent	Estimated volume per ha. m3 [2,3]	Growing stock	
			Million ha.[1]	Percent of total			Estimated total growing stock[4]	
							1,000 million m3	Percent of total
North America	1,875	700	260	11	37	90	23	9
Central America	272	71	36	1	51	85	3	1
South America	1,760	810	800	32	98	190	152	57
Africa	2,970	680	676	27	99	45	30	11
Europe	471	137	59	2	40	79	5	2
USSR	2,144	728	175	8	24	75	13	5
Asia	2,700	490	400	16	82	90	36	13
Pacific	842	88	84	3	95	58	5	2
World	13,034	3,704	2,490	100	67	712	267	100

[1]Includes mixed softwood and hardwood forest
[2]Including bark
[3]Derived from available estimates of growing stock for portions of the individual regions
[4]Derived by multiplying the estimated per hectare volume by area of hardwood forest

Source: Pringle [40], Pt. I, Table 6.

28

Table 3.2: Tropical Hardwood: Exports of Logs[1] and Processed Products[2] as Compared with Production of Logs, by Region, 1955 and 1968

(million m³(r))

	Year	Production of logs	Exports			Ratio of exports to Production %	Share of processed in exports %
			logs	processed	total		
Tropical Africa							
	1955	6.2	2.37	1.01	3.38	55	30
	1968	12.6	5.98	2.12	8.10	64	26
Increase in 1955-68		6.4	3.61	1.11	4.72		
Tropical Latin America							
	1955	15.8	0.39	0.36	0.74	5	49
	1968	16.5	0.40	0.92	1.32	8	70
Increase in 1955-68		0.7	0.01	0.56	0.58		
Tropical Asia-Pacific							
	1955	16.4	2.58	1.40	3.97	24	35
	1968	40.7	20.50	4.00	24.50	60	16
Increase in 1955-68		24.3	17.92	2.60	20.53		
Tropical Areas: Total							
	1955	38.4	5.34	2.77	8.11	21	34
	1968	69.8	26.88	7.04	33.92	49	21
Increase in 1955-68		31.4	21.54	4.27	25.81		

1"Logs" refer to sawlogs, veneer logs and logs for sleepers
2"Processed products" here refer to sawnwood, sleepers, veneer sheets and plywood

Source: FAO [20; 1955, 1968 eds.].

29

This paper also refers to "the *developing* Asia-Pacific region" which includes Korea and Taiwan as well as all of the tropical Asia-Pacific region and coincides with the "Developing Far East" plus "Developing Oceania" as defined in the *FAO Yearbook of Forest Products 1969-1970.*

Eighty percent of tropical industrial hardwood falls in the category of logs. The relative contribution of the three regions to world production and exports of logs as of 1968 is as follows (derived from Table 3.2):

		Exports	
	Production	Logs Only	Including Processed Products[2]
Tropical Africa	18.0%	22.2%	23.8%
Tropical Latin America	23.6%	1.4%	3.8%
Tropical Asia-Pacific	58.3%	76.2%	72.2%
Total	100.0%	100.0%	100.0%

It is clear that currently the most important source of tropical hardwood logs is tropical Asia-Pacific, which accounts for 58 percent of world production and 76 percent of log exports. Tropical Latin America is the second most important as a producer of logs but the least important as an exporter of logs because only less than 10 percent of what is produced there is exported (Table 3.2). Tropical Africa accounts for 18 percent of world production and 22 percent of the exports of logs (24 percent, if processed products are included).

In Table 3.2, exports of processed products (sawnwood, sleepers, veneers, and plywood), as measured in the roundwood equivalent volume, are shown together with exports of unprocessed logs. It is apparent that the rapid expansion in the production of tropical hardwood in Africa and in the Asia-Pacific region was led primarily by the phenomenal growth in exports from these regions. Total exports from all three regions increased from 8.1 million $m^3(r)$ in 1965 to 33.9 million $m^3(r)$ in 1968, or by 25.8 million $m^3(r)$ during the period. Eighty percent of this increase is accounted for by the Asia-Pacific region, and another 18 percent by Africa. Generally speaking, despite the allegedly vast reserves of tropical hardwood, Latin America has contributed very little to the growth of tropical hardwood trade. The following is a brief discussion of the exports and resources of tropical hardwood in each of the three regions.

Africa

Africa has 680 million hectares of forest, virtually all (99 percent) of which is hardwood forest. Some 180 million hectares of the forest are in

---

[2]Sawnwood, sleepers, veneers, and plywood.

the low altitude evergreen semideciduous belt in West and West Central Africa which supplies the bulk of timber exports.[3] The total growing stock of hardwood in Africa is estimated to be about 30 billion m^3.

Principal exporters, in order of importance, are the Ivory Coast (U.S.$104.3 million in 1968 exports of forest products), Gabon ($41.8 million), Ghana ($32.4 million), Congo [Brazzaville] ($25.5 million), Cameroon ($18.4 million), and Nigeria ($12.1 million). Other significant exporters with more than one million dollars of forest products exported in 1968 are Angola, Mozambique, Equatorial Guinea, Zaire, and the Central African Republic. Table 3.3 shows the exports of logs by major African countries together with major exporters in other regions.

An important feature of the tropical hardwood exports of Africa is that about 90 percent of the timber exports from tropical Africa, which have been expanding at about 8 percent per annum since the mid-1950s, are destined for Western Europe. It is partly because of the geographical proximity and partly because of the historical ties between some leading hardwood-consuming countries in Europe such as France and the United Kingdom on the one hand, and some leading wood producing countries in Africa such as the Ivory Coast, Cameroon, Gabon, Ghana, and Nigeria on the other. Another feature of tropical Africa's wood exports is the high and increasing ratio of exports to production, that is, about 55 percent even in the mid-1950s and almost 65 percent in the late 1960s. Undoubtedly the thriving exports have been the chief factor responsible for the expansion of hardwood log production in tropical Africa.

One of the important problems for the West African timber trade today is the fact that the standing volume of principal commercial species in demand is declining rapidly within the most accessible localities. The problem has broadly two aspects, the problem of species and the problem of location or accessibility.

In the virgin or older second-growth forest in West and West Central Africa the total density of the timber stand is said to be as high as 300 m^3 to the hectare, but only 80 m^3 are reported to be of the species that are potentially usable at the present time. Many African species that are available in sufficient quantities and suitable for industrial processing are not being exported at the present time because the merchants and the consumers in the importing countries lack confidence in less widely known species. It is reported that the volume actually harvested is between 5 and 20 m^3 per hectare, and rarely as much as 40 m^3 per hectare.[4]

Another problem for tropical Africa's hardwood exports is the prospective resource exhaustion in accessible localities of the region. The prob-

---

[3]Table 3.1 and Richardson [41].
[4]World Bank [57]. The case of Ghana is discussed in Richardson [41].

Table 3.3: Exports of Tropical Hardwood Logs[1] by Selected Countries, 1954, 1957, 1960, 1963, and 1965-71
(thousand cubic meters)

	1954	1957	1960	1963	1965	1966	1967	1968	1969	1970	1971
Asia-Pacific											
Burma	26	80	103	982	972	101	52	72	81	58	113
Indonesia	164	139	117	n.a.	140	203	502	1,879	3,685	7,834	9,899
Malaysia	n.a.	n.a.	n.a.	n.a.	6,038	8,192	9,035	10,514	11,111	11,353	11,140
West Malaysia	-[3]	2[3]	253	613	1,036	1,403	1,471	1,730	1,862	2,076	2,034
Sabah	451	954	1,723	3,001	3,796	4,856	5,321	5,796	6,187	6,150	6,558
Sarawak	156	147	349	875	1,206	1,933	2,243	2,988	3,061	3,128	2,548
Philippines	1,642	2,550	4,260	6,521	6,700	7,320[4]	7,950[4]	8,603[4]	11,027[4]	8,616	8,443
Thailand	13	22	36	21	28	37	31	29	29	30	64
New Guinea/Papua	-	11	7	67	67	120	181	103	79	155	424
British Solomon	-	-	-	4	19	32	80	126	206	227	255
Africa											
Cameroon	75	99	144	207	218	277	279	364	426	511	546
Congo (B.)	84	216	335	425	526	556	504	570	609	431	599
Congo (K.)	166	120	97	89	83	85	65	45	40[2]	34	342
Gabon	657	939	1,200	1,157	1,225	1,198	1,180	1,294	1,592	1,634	1,634[2]
Ghana	357	695	1,042	671	560	477	504	569	697	766	765[2]
Ivory Coast	n.a.	393	848	1,445	1,905	1,822	2,173	2,620	3,327	2,511	2,933
Nigeria	370	468	801	666	585	560	333	313	353	218	210
Latin America											
Brazil	59	60	55	44	53	58	79	117	114	84	119
Colombia	25	13	40	93	88	89	42	42	50	78	37
Paraguay	168	179	147	96	310	318	228	189	174	166	114

– Negligible
[1]SITC 242.3; sawlogs, veneer logs, and logs for sleepers
[2]Figures for the preceding years
[3]Net of exports to Singapore
[4]Based on importers' figures

Source: FAO [20; 1954-71 eds.].

lem seems to be most acute in Ghana and Nigeria where practically all high forest has been allocated on concessions and there are no unallocated tracts of forest within or outside reserves which are capable of sustaining major industrial units. It is believed to be impossible to maintain the current level of production on a *sustained* basis in the future unless a drastic change is introduced in the present forestry practices in these countries.[5] In the Ivory Coast, much of the accessible forest area has been lost to agriculture. Unlike Ghana and Nigeria, not all of the entire forest in this country is accessible and, so far, commercial fellings and extraction have been confined to the coastal strip. The hitherto closed forest of inland Ivory Coast could be made accessible if appropriate transportation facilities are provided. Similarly, recent restricted-circulation World Bank economic reports indicate that Gabon, Cameroon, Zaire, Congo (B.), Equatorial Guinea, and the CAR have a large area of closed forests which could be made accessible with improved transportation facilities. In fact, it is generally believed that the area of Western and Central Africa's closed forest that has not been commercially exploited is many times larger than the area of the forests that have been exhausted through exploitation.[6] If the hitherto inaccessible forests are made economically exploitable by infrastructural improvements, it seems unlikely that scarcity of commercial timber will force down exports from Western Africa within the next twenty years.[7]

The only hitherto-nonexporting country which may be capable of developing sizeable exports of tropical hardwood in Africa would be Liberia. Forest resources in Liberia are virtually untouched, only now beginning to be "opened up."

Latin America

Latin America is estimated to have over 830 million hectares of hardwood forest area containing a total growing stock of 155 billion m³ (Table 3.1). If these estimates are anywhere near the true magnitude, Latin America should have more than half of the world's total reserves of tropical hardwood. Yet, Latin America has never been an important source of tropical hardwood exports.[8] For the last two decades, production has been stagnant and exports have increased only modestly.

It is characteristic of the tropical hardwood trade of this region that a significant proportion of what little is exported by the surplus countries in

---

[5]Id. ut sup. [*Author's note:* see also ECA, *Forest Industries Development in West Africa* (New York: United Nations, 1966), pp. 47-50.]

[6]FAO [16], pp. 16-17.

[7]Ibid.

[8]A large part of Latin America's timber exports consist of the softwood exports from Brazil, Mexico, and a few other countries.

the region goes to other countries within the region.[9] For example, a large part of the timber exported from Paraguay goes to Argentina. Excluding much intraregional trade, main flows of the tropical hardwood exports from Latin America to outside the area are the exports of hardwood logs and sawnwood from Brazil, Colombia, and Ecuador to the United States and, in lesser quantities, to Japan and Canada. A relatively high portion of tropical hardwood exports of Latin America goes out in processed form.

Fundamental reasons for Latin America's disappointing failure to achieve more dynamic exports of tropical hardwood seem to be essentially two: (a) the extremely mixed specie composition of tropical hardwood forest in Latin America coupled with the relatively small average size of logs, which gives rise to formidable problems of market acceptance and utilization;[10] and (b) the extremely remote and inaccessible location of the apparently volume-rich forests, which contributes to the relatively high costs of exploitation in the region.[11]

The Asia-Pacific Region

From the viewpoint of tropical hardwood resources, the tropical Asia-Pacific region can be broadly divided into four parts: the Dipterocarp areas of mainland and insular Southeast Asia, the non-Dipterocarp area of the southwest Pacific islands, the teak forest area of Burma and Thailand, and the Indian subcontinent plus Ceylon.

Commercially, the Dipterocarp area is the most important of the four areas. It includes all of Indochina, the Philippines, Malaysia, and Indonesia west of the "Wallace Line" which separates the Malukus, Lesser Sunda Island, and West Irian from the rest of Indonesia. The non-Dipterocarp southwest Pacific islands include Indonesia east of the "Wallace Line," Papua/New Guinea, the Solomon Islands, and other tropical Pacific islands. Forests in Burma and Thailand are basically Dipterocarp forests but they contain teak resources. Burma and Thailand, along with Java of Indonesia, have been the important source of teakwood exports for a number of decades.

Timber trade in the tropical Asia-Pacific region has been dominated by exports of logs of Dipterocarpus and Shorea genera mainly from three countries, *the Philippines, Malaysia,* and *Indonesia.* These species are traded under such popular commercial names as lauans, apitongs, merantis ramin and keruing. The most important source of supply in the early 1950s was the Philippines, which was later joined by Malaysia (around

[9]See UNCTAD [51], especially Annex Tables 4 and 5.
[10]FAO [21], p. 46.
[11]ECLA/FAO/UNIDO [10], pp. 8-13.

1955-57). These two were most recently (after 1965) joined by Indonesia (see Table 3.3). The importance of these three countries is evidenced by the fact that they accounted for 97 percent of total exports from the region in 1969 (about 24.3 million m^3) and indeed 73 percent of total exports from all the tropical regions in that year (about 32.2 million m^3). Over 70 percent of the logs exported from the "big three" goes to Japan, and another 20 percent to 25 percent goes to Korea, Taiwan, and Singapore.

The recent growth of log exports from Indonesia has been so dramatic that it deserves a special mention. Exports rose from 1.2 million m^3(r) in 1968 to over 10 million m^3(r) in 1970. This sudden rise of log exports is primarily due to the logging boom in Kalimantan. The log exports from the non-Dipterocarp area of Indonesia, that is, the islands east of the "Wallace Line" including West Irian, are still relatively small.

The Philippines and Malaysia have well-established timber processing industries but Indonesia does not. The Philippines exports respectable volumes of plywood and veneer sheets (together about 470 thousand m^3 in 1968) as well as significant quantities of sawnwood (100-170 thousand m^3(s) in recent years). Malaysia is a leading exporter of sawnwood (1.2 million m^3(s) per annum in 1968-69, including some sleepers). Three-quarters of the exports come from West Malaysia and most of the rest from Sarawak. In addition, Malaysia (mainly West Malaysia) exports over 100 thousand m^3 of plywood.

Forest resources in the southwest Pacific islands are reportedly rich in volume but are of non-Dipterocarp species, most of which are not yet known to the major end markets. The mixed and varied specie composition presents a formidable marketing problem. Currently, a little over 300 thousand m^3(r) of logs are exported—two-thirds from *the Solomon Islands* and one-third from *Papua/New Guinea.* Many of the species found in Papua/New Guinea are also found in the Solomon Islands. The species distribution in the latter, however, is said to be more favorable for exploitation than that found in Papua/New Guinea.

Indochina has basically Dipterocarp-type resources. But the lack of political stability in Cambodia, Laos, and Vietnam has limited the scale of timber exports from these countries. However, given political stability in this area, about half a million m^3(r) of logs could be made available for export from Cambodia, either in log or processed form.[12] On the other hand, export prospects from Laos and Vietnam are very uncertain at the present time.

Along with the Java island of Indonesia, Thailand and Burma have traditionally been the most important source of *teakwood.* Current exports of

---

[12]Tuolumne Corporation [49], p. 65.

teakwood from these three sources are about 350 thousand m³(r). The most important source is Burma, which accounts for 70 percent of the region's total teak exports (in roundwood equivalent volume). She has suffered chronic production problems and, according to a restricted-circulation report by the 1972 World Bank economic mission to Burma, these are expected to continue as long as political problems keep some of the best teak forests in the hands of insurgents.[13] A 1972 World Bank report on Thailand's agricultural sector notes that that nation's supply position is believed to be critical as a result of over-cutting in earlier periods. Unless steps are taken to restrict the local use of teak, Thailand's exports of teak will tend to decline. Indonesia, according to another World Bank sector mission report, has shown steady growth in teak exports.

About 90 percent of the estimated production of industrial wood (about 10 million m³ in 1968) in the *Indian Subcontinent and Ceylon* is hardwood. Almost all is consumed in the domestic market. This region is not expected to become a major exporter of tropical hardwood.

---

[13]The current Four Year Plan aims at 11 percent increase in teak exports by the 1974/75 fiscal year.

IV: Markets for Tropical Hardwood: Trends and Prospects

This chapter reviews the broad trends in world trade and consumption of tropical hardwood and discusses the demand outlook. World annual consumption of tropical hardwood increased from 38.6 million $m^3(r)$ to 71.3 million $m^3(r)$ in the thirteen-year period from 1955 to 1968 at 4.8 percent per annum. Consumption in the importing areas rose much faster than that in the producing areas. Consumption in the importing areas increased at 12.3 percent per annum from 7.3 million $m^3(r)$ in 1955 to 33.2 million $m^3(r)$ in 1968, while consumption in the producing areas advanced from 31.3 million $m^3(r)$ to 38.1 million $m^3(r)$, that is, only at 1.5 percent per annum over the same period. As a result of the different rates of growth in consumption between the two regions, the relative share of the importing areas in world consumption of tropical hardwood increased from approximately 20 percent in 1955 to 47 percent in 1968.

Among the principal areas importing tropical hardwood are Japan, Western Europe, and the United States. Besides these and other developed countries, some developing countries—Korea, Taiwan, Singapore, and others—import a significant volume of tropical hardwood in log form and "re-export" most of it after processing it into plywood, sawnwood, and veneers. Net domestic consumption in these countries has been growing, but has not yet reached a significant scale. The CPEs also import some tropical hardwood. The growth in tropical hardwood consumption in the major importing areas as well as in the major producing areas is shown in Table 4.1 (along with projections which will be discussed later).

Table 4.1: Projected Demand for Tropical Hardwood, by Major Areas, up to 1985[1]

(unit: million m³(r))

	Actual[2]				Projected			Implied Growth Rates		
	1955	1960	1965	1968	1975	1980	1985	1965-75	1968-75	1975-85
								(percent per annum)		
Tropical Producing Areas	31.3	30.6	35.1	38.1	46.3	53.2	61.0	2.8	2.8	2.8
Tropical Africa	3.1	3.5	3.8	4.3	n.a.	n.a.	n.a.			
Tropical Latin America	15.2	13.9	15.5	15.4	n.a.	n.a.	n.a.			
Tropical Asia	13.0	13.2	15.9	18.4	n.a.	n.a.	n.a.			
Importing Areas[3]	7.3	14.2	22.8	33.2	54.5	69.5	83.1	9.1	7.3	4.3
Europe	3.5	6.2	8.4	10.0	12.0	13.0	14.0	3.6	2.6	1.6
United States	1.4	2.0	3.2	6.4	10.9	14.3	16.0	13.0	7.9	3.9
Japan	1.3	4.1	9.2	13.7	28.0	37.5	47.0	11.8	10.8	5.3
Rest of the world	1.1	1.9	2.1	3.1	3.6	4.7	6.0	5.5	2.2	5.4
World Total	38.6	44.8	57.9	71.3	100.8	122.7	144.0	5.7	5.1	3.6

[1]Regional figures may not add to totals because of rounding
[2]Three-year averages, except for 1968
[3]Consumption in all areas outside the tropical areas

Source: Actual 1955-1968 compiled from published reports by FAO, OECD, U.S. Department of Commerce, and Japan Ministry of Finance; projected 1975-1985 estimates from the World Bank Economic Analysis and Projections Department.

Table 4.2: Exports of Tropical Hardwood Sawnwood by Selected Countries, by Destination, 1968
(unit: 1,000 m³(s))

Exporters/Destinations	Total Exports	Japan	Singapore	United States	Canada	Australia	Western Europe EEC	U.K.	Other	Total	South Africa	Rest of the world
Asia												
Burma	100	0.7	16.1	—	0.5	0.5	7.6	11.3	23.9	42.8	—	39.4
Philippines	103	18.4	—	53.0	0.1	9.3	0.8	—	4.8	5.6	14.4	1.7
Singapore	556	34.2	—	23.2	10.8	31.0	122.4	16.4	48.1	186.9	75.8	194.1
Malaysia												
West Malaysia	843	81.3	176.0	51.7	18.9	123.2	177.1	92.7	9.2	279.0	48.3	64.7
Sarawak	311	1.1	—	33.4	0.1	29.0	121.8	70.4	9.8	202.0	0.4	45.0
Total	1,154	82.4	176.0	85.1	19.0	152.2	298.9	163.1	19.0	481.0	48.7	109.7
Africa												
Ghana	215	0.2	—	20.8	1.4	0.5	26.1	135.1	14.5	175.7	—	16.4
Ivory Coast	188	—	—	11.0	1.3	—	79.3	67.8	13.2	160.3	—	27.7
Latin America												
Brazil	82	—	—	50.9	0.1	—	4.7	1.6	7.2	13.5	11.4	6.3
Colombia	104	2.0	—	58.2	18.2	—	21.5	1.7	—	23.2	—	2.6

Source: FAO [20; 1970 ed.], Table D11 supplemented by Table D12.

The Growth of Trade in Processed Tropical Hardwood

As discussed at the beginning of Chapter III, exports of processed tropical hardwood from the producing regions have been increasing rapidly (at 6.5 percent per annum in 1955-1968; see Table 3.2). In roundwood equivalent terms, sawnwood has been the most important form; plywood, the second; and veneers, the least important.

Among the log-exporting countries in the tropical Asia-Pacific region, Malaysia (West Malaysia and Sarawak) and, to a lesser extent, the Philippines, are the most important sawnwood exporters (Table 4.2). Singapore is a major in-transit processor-exporter of sawnwood. Direction of world trade in tropical hardwood sawnwood as of 1968 is shown in Table 4.2.

World exports of tropical hardwood plywood have been expanding rapidly. Due to lack of detailed data, it is not possible to estimate the total exports of tropical hardwood plywood in early years. World exports of plywood (all species) increased from 0.53 million m^3 in 1953 to 4.30 million m^3 in 1969. During the same period, plywood exports from the Far East (excluding CPEs) and the Pacific increased from 0.10 million m^3 to 2.21 million m^3; virtually all of these are made of tropical hardwood.

An important trend in world exports of tropical hardwood plywood is the predominant role played by Asian countries, especially by log-importing processor-exporters. The pioneer was Japan in the 1950s; she has been shipping the product principally to the U.S. market. Japan exports so-called lauan (or Philippine mahogany) plywood, domestic species plywood and specialty plywood; the latter two use tropical hardwood except for the face ply. The "domestic species plywood" uses domestic species such as birch and sen as the face ply, while the "specialty plywood" has a special face finish, that is, laminated finish, printed finish, and the like. Japanese plywood exports as a whole increased rapidly—for example, at about 8 percent per annum in 1955-1959—but have been stagnating since 1959. The stagnation was mainly due to the increased competition in the U.S. market and the rapid expansion of the domestic market in Japan. Towards the end of the 1950s, Taiwan and Korea, following the steps of Japan and based similarly on the logs imported from the Philippines, began to export lauan plywood principally to the U.S. market. They rapidly built up their exports in the 1960s, displacing Japan's lauan plywood exports to the U.S. market, although Japan continued her expansion of exports of other categories of plywood. Singapore is another significant in-transit exporter of plywood.

In the meantime, the log-producing Philippines also built up the lauan plywood exports beginning in the late 1950s and soon became a major exporter of hardwood plywood in the Pacific Basin although her exports of

Table 4.3 : Direction of Trade in Hardwood Plywood,[1] Selected Exporting Areas, by Destination, 1969
(unit: thousand cubic meters)

From/To	Total	United States	Canada	United Kingdom	EEC	Hong Kong	Australia	Others Unknown
Taiwan	596	403	94	1	—	26	8	64
Korea, Republic of	709	684	4	—	—	—	—	21
Malaysia	109	41	2	34	—	5	—	27
Philippines	249	246	—	—	—	3	—	—
Singapore	110	8	5	29	1	2	—	65
Japan	402	317	34	27	9	1	8	6
Other Asia	19	12	—	4	2	—	—	1
Southwest Pacific Islands	12	—	—	—	—	—	12	—
Africa	126	1	—	50	43	—	1	31
Israel	56	1	—	33	1	—	—	21
Latin America	50	7	1	8	2	—	—	32
Total	2,438	1,720	140	153	58	37	29	268

[1]Practically all are tropical hardwood

Source: FAO [20; 1970 ed.], Table D16. Totals for the Philippines, Japan and Southwest Pacific Islands have been adjusted for consistency, on the basis of other trade tables in the *Yearbook.*

plywood have been stagnating lately. Almost all of the Philippines' exports go to the U.S. market, where she has enjoyed the benefit of preferential tariffs since 1963. Plywood exports of Malaysia (so far, mostly West Malaysia) are also significant and growing; their main destinations have been the United Kingdom and North America. Exports of tropical hardwood plywood from major exporters to major destinations in 1969 are indicated in Table 4.3.

Exports of tropical hardwood in veneer form have been expanding steadily. The largest exporter is the Philippines which exported about 250 thousand m^3 accounting for almost half of the total exports by all developing countries. In Asia, non-log-producing Singapore has recently been increasing veneer exports. Major exporters and importers are shown in Table 4.4.

The rapid growth of export trade in processed tropical hardwood in the Far East in the last two decades can be largely explained by three factors: in the case of Japan, Korea, and Taiwan, the extremely export-oriented industrial strategy of these countries; in the case of the Philippines, the preferential tariff arrangement in the U.S. market; and in the case of Malaysia and Singapore, the export-oriented, outward-looking policies of these countries plus the advantages of the Commonwealth preferences.

Demand in the United States

Consumption of tropical hardwood in the United States has been growing rapidly for the last two decades. Consumption rose at an average rate of 8.3 percent per annum in the period from the mid-1950s to the mid-1960s, and has since continued to increase at an even faster rate.

The United States imports hardwood (mostly tropical) in the form of plywood, sawnwood, and veneer rather than in the form of logs. In 1968, for example, plywood accounted for 70 percent of the total hardwood imports of 7.8 million m^3 (net imports 6.8 million m^3) measured in roundwood equivalent, while sawnwood and veneer accounted for a further 20 percent and 8 percent, respectively.[1] U.S. imports of hardwood logs have always been small and have tended to decline since the mid-1950s. These are not expected to increase significantly.

Following the trend of the 1950s, imports of hardwood plywood by the United States continued to expand very rapidly in the 1960s, rising from 6 million m^2 (surface measures) in the 1960-61 period to 481 million m^2 in 1971 (Table 4.5). Almost all the increase was accounted for by tropical

---

[1]Hair [23].

Table 4.4: Exports of Veneer Sheets[1] (All Species) by Developing Countries 1968

(unit: 1,000m³)

	Total Exports	Destinations		
		United States	Western Europe	Other Area
Latin America	43.1	n.a.	n.a.	n.a.
Brazil	29.8	24.4	3.0	2.4
Africa	134.8	n.a.	n.a.	n.a.
Cameroon	30.0	n.a.	n.a.	n.a.
Congo (B.)	55.0	12.7	7.7	34.6
Congo (K.)	14.4	n.a.	n.a.	n.a.
Gabon	9.6	0.1	8.5	1.0
Ivory Coast	24.9	8.0	13.7	3.2
Asia-Pacific	301.3	191.2	n.a.	n.a.
Malaysia	20.0	6.9	—	13.1
Philippines	219.6	134.8	—	84.8
Singapore	59.8	49.5	0.1	10.2
Total[2]	479	292	57	130

[1]Virtually all are of tropical hardwood
[2]Rounded

Source: Based on FAO [20; 1970 ed.], Tables T2 and D13, supplemented by Table D14.

hardwood plywood, which in turn was mostly lauan plywood.[2] The imports of hardwood veneer in the United States also have been increasing rapidly at an average rate exceeding 10 percent during the 1960s although they constitute only a minor part of the total hardwood imports in the United States. The share of tropical species in the hardwood veneer imports has been increasing. Tropical species now account for almost 60 percent of all hardwood veneer imports. Most of the increases in imports of hardwood plywood and veneer, then, have been in tropical species, which now account for 90 percent of the total imports; these increases have been largely in Southeast Asian species.

According to a recent study by the Forest Service of the U.S. Department of Agriculture,[3] the United States's demand for hardwood plywood and veneer is projected to increase from 455 million m² (9.5 mm basis) in 1968 to 743 million m² in 1985, that is, at an annual rate of 3 percent. The study also suggests that most of the projected increase in demand will be

[2]Large and growing quantities of "birch plywood," "sen-plywood," and other "specialty plywoods" have been imported from Japan. However, these "nontropical" hardwood plywoods normally use lauan and similar Southeast Asian hardwoods for the cores and back plies.

[3]Hair [23].

43

Table 4.5: U.S. Imports of Hardwood[1] Plywood, by Country of Origin, 1955-72
(unit: million square meters, surface measure)

Year	Asia						Latin America	Africa	Canada	Europe	Other	World Total
	Japan	Taiwan	Korea	Philippines	Other	Sub-Total						
1955	39.8	—	—	0.9	—	40.8	0.8	1.0	9.2	5.8	0.6	58.3
1956	49.0	—	—	1.4	—	50.5	0.5	1.3	7.5	5.0	0.9	65.6
1957	63.2	—	—	3.1	—	66.7	0.9	1.0	6.0	3.8	0.4	78.6
1958	62.2	2.2	—	9.0	0.4	73.8	1.1	1.4	3.9	4.3	0.1	84.7
1959	75.3	3.5	—	19.8	1.9	100.6	3.0	2.4	5.6	11.6	0.4	123.6
1960	63.9	4.2	—	11.0	0.4	79.6	1.3	1.6	4.0	7.7	—	94.2
1961	61.4	10.1	1.5	14.3	2.2	89.4	1.6	1.4	3.9	5.4	0.1	101.9
1962	68.8	19.7	4.8	19.9	4.7	117.9	1.4	1.3	5.3	7.8	0.2	133.7
1963	68.7	25.4	11.2	22.9	4.5	132.7	1.7	0.8	6.7	8.6	—	150.6
1964	63.2	42.9	19.1	33.0	4.1	162.3	1.3	0.9	6.3	10.1	—	180.9
1965	71.3	43.5	31.3	28.6	4.8	179.5	1.0	0.6	6.0	11.0	—	198.1
1966	72.8	49.1	53.3	37.0	4.2	216.4	0.8	0.6	6.0	13.5	—	237.2
1967	58.7	45.1	65.2	43.8	6.0	218.9	0.8	0.2	4.5	11.0	—	235.3
1968	85.6	77.1	108.4	55.9	9.2	336.2	1.1	0.1	4.9	14.5	—	356.8
1969	74.5	87.0	147.7	53.1	13.3	375.7	1.1	0.2	3.8	17.9	—	398.6
1970	57.9	87.3	166.0	53.0	7.0	371.3	1.0	0.5	2.3	12.6	—	387.2
1971	55.7	129.9	209.3	55.1	14.1	464.1	1.3	—	4.2	11.8	—	481.4
1972	48.1	187.6	9.9	59.2	271.2	576.0	2.0	0.0	6.1	11.1	—	595.2

[1]Includes mixed species (not classified as hardwoods or softwoods)

Source: U.S. Dept. of Agriculture [53]; U.S. Dept. of Commerce [54, 1972 ed.].

supplied by imports. Most of the increases in imports will be of tropical species. We estimate that the U.S. imports of tropical hardwood in the forms of plywood and veneer would rise at 7.5 percent per annum between 1968 and 1975, at 5 percent between 1975 and 1980, and at 1.5 percent between 1980 and 1985. Imports of tropical hardwood in the form of plywood and veneer would thus rise from 240 million m² (9.5 mm basis) in 1968 to 400 million m² by 1975, to 510 million m² by 1980, and to 550 million m² by 1985.

Hardwood sawnwood imports of the United States rose at about 3 percent per annum between 1950-54 and 1965-69, from 587 thousand m³(s) per annum to 892 thousand m³(s) per annum.[4] The largest single source has been Canada, which accounted for 40 percent to 45 percent during the last 15 years or so. Canada's share has not changed in any systematic way. All imports from Canada are temperate hardwoods. Between 1954-56 and 1966-68, Asia's share fell from 41 percent to 27 percent, while Latin America's share increased from 11 percent to 21 percent and that of Africa also increased slightly from 5 percent to 7 percent during the same period. The United States's imports of *tropical hardwood* sawnwood from all sources in 1968 are estimated to have been 440 thousand m³(s), or 54 percent of total hardwood sawnwood imports in that year. Asia supplied 230 thousand m³(s), while Latin America and Africa supplied 170 and 43 thousand m³(s), respectively.

Consumption of hardwood sawnwood in the United States is projected to increase from 16.8 million m³(s) in 1968 to 24.8 million m³(s) in 1980, or at 3.3 percent per year.[5] About 60 percent of the projected demand increase, however, will be in the average—or lower—quality hardwood sawnwood, which may be essentially met by increased supplies from the domestic hardwood resources.[6] The U.S. domestic hardwood supply situation has improved over the last decade or so. The U.S. Forest Service estimates that, if recent trends in intensive forest management continue in the future, the domestic supply of hardwood timber of less preferred species or of lower quality species or both will increase over the next couple of decades, and that "most of the additional demand for lumber (sawnwood) and perhaps some of the demand for veneer and plywood could be met by use of the timber currently available and the additional growth expected in the years immediately ahead."[7] Consequently, only a small part of the projected increase in demand for hardwood sawnwood

---

[4]U.S. Department of Commerce figures given in million board feet have been converted to figures in thousand cubic meters by using the FAO-recommended conversion factor of 2.36 m³(s) = 1,000 board feet.

[5]Hair [23] gives figures in billion board feet.

[6]Tuolumne Corporation [48], p. 79.

[7]Hair and Spada [24].

should be expected to be met by increased imports even if an allowance is made for the possibility that "recent trends in intensive forest management" may not continue exactly as the U.S. Forest Service expects. Assuming (a) that all of the additional demand for average-to-lower quality sawnwood (60 percent of the projected 8 million m^3 increase) and as much as two-thirds of the additional demand for better-quality sawnwood would be met by domestic supply over the period up to 1980, and (b) that tropical hardwood would gradually increase its share in total hardwood imports, imports of tropical hardwood sawnwood might be projected to increase from 440 thousand $m^3(s)$ in 1968 to 1.4 million $m^3(s)$ by 1980, or at 10 percent per annum.

In summary, it is estimated that U.S. imports of tropical hardwood could rise from 6.4 million $m^3(r)$ in 1968 to 10.9 million $m^3(r)$ by 1975, to 14.3 million $m^3(r)$ by 1980, and to 16 million $m^3(r)$ by 1985 (Table 4.1). The implied growth rate for the 1968-80 period is 6.9 percent per annum.

Demand in Japan

Japan has been by far the most important market for tropical hardwood exports of the tropical Asia-Pacific region. Japan's annual consumption of tropical hardwood expanded from 1.3 million $m^3(r)$ in the mid-1950s to 13.7 million $m^3(r)$ in 1968 (Table 4.1), and to over 20 million $m^3(r)$ in 1971. During 1971, Japan imported almost 21 million $m^3(r)$ of tropical hardwood logs together with a little less than 0.75 million m^3 (roundwood equivalent) of processed hardwood. During the same year, she exported some 83 million m^2 of plywood which represented about 0.6 million m^3 (roundwood equivalent) of tropical hardwood.

Japan has been importing most of her tropical hardwood in the form of logs. Her imports of tropical hardwood logs increased from 1.9 million $m^3(r)$ in 1955 to 21.0 million $m^3(r)$ in 1971 (Table 4.6). Ninety-nine percent of tropical hardwood logs have been imported from tropical Asia. Major sources have been the Philippines and Malaysia, and recently Indonesia as well. As of 1971, Indonesia, the Philippines, and Malaysia accounted for 39 percent, 29 percent, and 28 percent of total tropical hardwood log imports in Japan respectively.

It is only in recent years that Japan's imports of processed tropical hardwood have increased (Table 4.7). In 1970, imports of *sawnwood* amounted to 265 thousand $m^3(s)$; 90 percent was of Dipterocarpaceae species. West Malaysia was the major supplier. *Veneer* imports amounted to 5.4 million m^2 (surface measure) in 1967, exceeding U.S.$1 million in value for the first time, and subsequently increased to 14 million m^2 (surface measure) in 1970. The major sources of supply are the Philip-

Table 4.6: Japan's Imports of Logs,[1] by Geographical Sources, and by Species, 1954-72
(unit: 1,000 m³)

	Tropical Hardwood Logs						Total Imports[2]	Softwood Log Imports[3]	Total Logs Hardwood & Softwood[4]	% of Tropical Hardwood in All Logs
	Malaya & Singapore	Sabah	Sarawak	Indonesia	Philippines	Tropical Africa				
1954	—	148	—	11	1,302	—	1,464	272	1,764	83.0
1955	—	172	—	15	1,661	—	1,858	102	1,966	94.5
1956	—	235	—	17	2,061	—	2,320	155	2,486	93.3
1957	—	355	1	10	2,093	—	2,165	251	2,433	88.9
1958	—	561	11	5	2,758	1	3,342	570	3,950	84.6
1959	43	903	79	9	3,309	3	4,370	971	5,355	81.6
1960	22	1,051	106	12	3,472	5	4,729	1,233	5,984	79.0
1961	1	1,698	211	9	3,818	10	5,813	2,672	8,529	68.2
1962	—	1,863	224	11	4,460	5	6,637	3,161	9,844	67.4
1963	40	2,131	364	32	5,488	4	8,200	4,320	12,558	65.3
1964	72	2,267	424	110	5,284	9	8,292	5,354	13,683	60.6
1965	86	2,789	605	124	5,612	9	9,343	5,947	15,374	60.8
1966	116	3,501	1,233	178	6,716	148	12,068	7,559	19,744	61.1
1967	281	3,897	1,461	468	7,174	150	13,689	11,478	25,265	54.2
1968	174	3,752	1,931	898	7,310	30	14,480	15,578	30,058	48.2
1969	156	4,031	2,032	2,357	8,167	91	17,190	15,545	32,735	52.5
1970	189	3,944	1,874	5,484	7,700	48	19,785	18,395	38,245	51.7
1971	169	4,160	1,537	8,199	6,139	66	20,997	12,699	33,743	62.2
1972	177	5,296	1,431	8,503	5,146	76	21,333	19,795	41,132	51.9
1954-56—Average	—	185	—	14	1,675	—	1,880	176	2,070	90.8
1959-61 "	22	1,217	132	10	3,531	6	4,971	1,625	6,616	75.1
1964-66 "	91	2,852	754	137	5,871	55	9,901	6,287	16,251	60.9
1969-71 "	171	4,045	1,814	5,347	7,335	68	19,324	15,546	34,908	55.4

1"Logs" in this table means sawlogs, veneer logs, and logs for sleepers
2Includes log imports from other tropical areas
3SITC 242.2. Includes tropical softwood
4SITC 242.2 + SITC 242.3. Includes temperate hardwoods

Source: Japan, Ministry of Finance [28; 1954-72 eds.].

Table 4.7: Japan's Imports of Processed Tropical Hardwood, 1961-65, 1966-71

Product	Unit	1961-65 average	1966	1967	1968	1969	1970	1971
Sawnwood[1]	1,000 m³(s)	10	39	130	132	174	260	236
Sleepers	1,000 m³(s)	n.a.	n.a.	n.a.	n.a.	31	36	39
Veneer sheets[2]	million m²	n.à.	0.4	5.4	6.5	6.8	15.5	23.9
Plywood[3]	million m²	0.04	0.4	5.3	0.9	6.6	63.8	14.0

[1]Figures up to 1969 include all tropical hardwood; figures for 1970 and 1971 include only "South Seas" sawnwood, thus leaving out teak as well as other tropical species of non-Asian origin which amount to about 5 percent of total

[2]Includes about 5 percent of nontropical species, except for the figure for 1971

[3]Includes about one percent of nontropical species, except for the figure for 1971

Source: Japan, Ministry of Finance [28], Ministry of Agriculture & Forestry [30]; Japan South Seas Lumber Association; FAO [20].

pines, Malaysia and Singapore, which together account for more than 90 percent of the Japanese veneer imports. *Plywood* imports, in response to a severe shortage in the domestic market, spiralled in a massive scale in 1970, amounting to 63.6 million m² (surface measure) worth U.S.$30 million, against 6.6 million m² (surface measure) imported in 1969. Most of plywood imports came from Taiwan and Korea in 1970.

In addition to tropical hardwood, Japan imports vast quantities of *temperate softwood,* again largely in the form of logs. Softwood accounts for about half of total log imports in Japan. Her imports of softwood logs amounted to 15.6 million m³(r) in 1968, accounting for 70 percent of the world's total imports of softwood logs. The main sources of supply have been the United States (mostly the Pacific Northwest), the USSR (Siberia), and Canada (primarily British Columbia). Recently New Zealand has also become an important source of softwood logs for Japan. The United States (hemlock, Douglas fir, and others) and the USSR (spruce and pine) together account for over 85 percent of Japan's total imports of softwood (logs and sawnwood combined).

Consumption of industrial wood (all species) in Japan has been expanding at about 6 percent per annum over the last decade, and is estimated to have reached 100 million m³ in 1970 (Table 4.8). Currently, about 45 percent of the requirements is met by domestic supply while the remaining 55 percent is met by imports. In every major use the share of imported wood material has been increasing in the last two decades. In plywood production, well over 90 percent of wood material used is now imported and mostly of tropical species. In sawnwood production, which uses 60 percent of total industrial wood in Japan, the share of imported

48

wood raw material rose from less than 20 percent in 1962 to almost 50 percent in 1969.

Projections of demand for and supply of industrial wood (all species) in Japan in 1980 and 1981 are presented in Table 4.8. The estimates for total demand, domestic supply (alternative I) and import demand (alternative I) for the year 1981 are the latest estimates made by the Forestry Agency of Japan. The estimate for domestic supply in 1981 (alternative I) assumes that the new "Basic Plan Regarding Forest Resource" recommended by the Forest Agency will be fully implemented on schedule. Therefore, it should be construed as the maximum possible domestic supply in 1981, and the alternative II import demand estimate as the minimum import requirements in 1981. Alternative II estimates for domestic supply and import demand for 1981 are those made by the author on the basis of the assumption that domestic supply will probably continue to decrease in the next decade as the historical experience with forest improvement plans in Japan shows. All projections for 1980 have been derived by interpolation.

Japan's total demand for industrial wood is projected to increase from about 92 million $m^3(r)$ in 1968 to about 131 million $m^3(r)$ by 1980. Domestic supply is likely to decrease from 49 million $m^3(r)$ in 1968 to 44 million $m^3(r)$ by 1980 (the alternative II projection) and import demand will increase from 43 million $m^3(r)$ in 1968 to 88 million $m^3(r)$ by 1980.

Table 4.8: Japan: Projected Domestic Supply of and Total Demand and Import Demand for Industrial Wood (All Species), 1980 and 1981
(unit: million $m^3(r)$)

	Actual		Estimated	
	1968	1969-71 (average)	1980	1981
Demand				
Wood for sawnwood	59.0	60.4	(70.1)	71.6
Wood for plywood	8.9	12.3	(19.7)	20.5
Wood for pulp	20.2	23.5	(38.3)	40.1
Wood for other purposes	3.7	3.6	(2.7)	2.6
Total demand	91.8	99.9	(130.8)	134.8
Supply				
Domestic supply				
Alternative I	48.9	46.3	(49.2)	49.7
Alternative II	48.9	46.3	(44.0)	n.a.
Imports				
Alternative I	42.9	53.6	(82.5)	85.1
Alternative II	42.9	53.6	(87.7)	n.a.
Total supply	91.8	99.9	(131.7)	·134.8

Source: Japan, Ministry of Agriculture and Forestry [29], p. 44; author's estimates.

49

Assuming that the share of tropical hardwood in the total imports of wood used for sawnwood remains the same as in the 1968-70 period, and that most of the wood required for plywood will continue to be tropical hardwood, Japanese tropical hardwood consumption[8] is projected to rise from about 20 million $m^3(r)$ in 1970 to 37.5 million $m^3(r)$ in 1980.

Demand in Europe

Europe is another important market for tropical hardwood. It is difficult to know exactly how much tropical hardwood is "consumed" in Europe because of the existence of intraregional trade within Europe. Roughly speaking, tropical hardwood consumption in Europe is estimated to have increased from 3.5 million $m^3(r)$ in the mid-1950s to around 10.0 million $m^3(r)$ in the late 1960s—in other words, at the rate of about 8 percent per annum. Growth in Europe's consumption has been rather slow in the last few years.

About 70 percent of Europe's tropical hardwood imports are in the form of logs, a little less than 30 percent in the form of sawnwood, and the rest (2 percent to 3 percent) in the form of veneers and plywood. An overwhelming part of Europe's imports have been of African origin. Recently, however, because of growing imports from the Asia-Pacific region, the proportion of imports from Africa has decreased to about 75 percent.

Sawnwood imports by Europe from the Asia-Pacific region are especially important. In 1969, seven major West European importing countries—the United Kingdom, France, Federal Republic of Germany, Netherlands, Belgium, Luxembourg, Denmark, and Italy—imported about 1.36 million $m^3(s)$ of tropical hardwood sawnwood; 60 percent of these, 0.81 million $m^3(s)$, came from four Asian countries, namely, Malaysia, Singapore, Burma, and Thailand.[9] In the same year, the seven major West European countries imported about 0.5 million $m^3(r)$ of logs from the Asia-Pacific region. Similarly, Europe (excluding the USSR) imported about 116 thousand m^3 of tropical hardwood plywood from the Asia-Pacific region in 1969.[10]

Table 4.9 shows the projected consumption and domestic supply of industrial wood in Europe (excluding the USSR) up to 1980 in terms of wood raw material equivalent (WRME),[11] as estimated by T.J. Peck of the

---

[8]Apparent consumption equals the imports of logs and processed timber minus exports in the form of plywood (roundwood equivalent). Japanese exports of tropical timber in the form of plywood are expected to remain at their current level with, at best, only minor fluctuations in coming years.

[9]ECE/FAO [6].

[10]ECE/FAO [9], XXIII(4):80-81.

[11]Figures in wood raw material equivalent (WRME) include roundwood equivalent of wood residues consumed in the production of particle board, fiberboard and wood pulp. Thus, the total consumption figures double count the residues used in these industries.

50

Table 4.9: Europe: Forest Products Balance,[1] 1950-70, and Estimates, 1980-2000

(million m³ WRME)

	Actual			Fore-cast	Tentative Forecasts			
	1950	1960	1970	1980	1990		2000	
					Low	High	Low	High
All forest products								
Consumption	298	346	475	519	590	650	640	780
Total supply, of which	295	341	415					
Removals	294	312	345	400	410	450	420	480
Transfer of residues	5	13	27	40	50	60	55	70
Net imports	(4)[2]	15	43					
Apparent shortfall[3]				79	130	140	165	230
Sawlogs, veneer logs and their products								
Consumption	103	138	172	198	200	210	190	210
Total supply, of which	101	133	171					
Removals	100	118	145	165	170	180	180	190
Net imports	1	15	26					
Apparent shortfall[3]				33	30	30	10	20
Pulpwood and its products								
Consumption	37	74	142	245	330	390	400	540
Total supply, of which	36	76	138					
Removals	37	60	95	160	180	220	190	260
Transfer of residues	5	13	27	40	50	60	55	70
Net imports	(6)[2]	3	16					
Apparent shortfall[3]				45	100	110	155	210
Other forest products (incl. fuelwood)								
Consumption	158	134	101	76	60	50	50	30
Total supply, of which	158	134	106					
Removals	157	134	105	75	60	50	50	30
Net imports	1	—	1					
Apparent shortfall[3]	—	—	—	—	—	—	—	—

[1]The fact that total supply does not always exactly balance with consumption can be attributed to a number of factors, the most important of which are imprecise conversion factors and incorrect classification, particularly of roundwood removals

[2]Net exports

[3]The difference between the estimates of consumption and those of removals and transfer of residues (where applicable); thus, estimates of net import requirements

Source: Peck [38], Table 11.

joint Timber Division of the UN Economic Commission for Europe and the FAO.[12] Consumption of sawnwood, plywood, and veneers is projected to increase from 172 million m^3WRME in 1970 to 198 million m^3WRME in 1980 — that is, at about 1.5 percent per year. In the meantime, European production or log removal (excluding the USSR) is estimated to rise from 145 million m^3(r) in 1970 to 165 million m^3(r) in 1980, with the result that the net imports of logs and their products would increase from 26 million m^3(r) to 33 million m^3(r) in the 1970-80 period.

Imports of hardwood logs, and hardwood sawnwood, plywood, and veneers in Europe were projected to increase by 3 to 4 million m^3(r) between 1965 and 1980 by the ECE/FAO Timber Division.[13] Events since the underlying study was carried out appear to justify the use of the figure at the top of this range. Assuming that all of the additional imports of hardwood in this category will be of tropical origin, consumption of tropical hardwood in Europe has been projected to increase from around 10 million m^3(r) in 1968 to 13 million m^3(r) in 1980 (see Table 4.1).

Consumption of other industrial wood in Europe is expected to rise much faster than that of logs in the 1965-80 period (Table 4.9). Although domestic supply is expected to increase, the apparent shortfall is also expected to increase, from 7 million m^3WRME in 1965 to 38 million m^3WRME in 1980.[14]

World Demand Prospects

Projected world demand for tropical hardwood for the period up to 1985 is summarized in Table 4.1.

One general conclusion that may be drawn from the projections is that demand for tropical hardwood outside the tropical producing areas as a whole would continue to grow rather rapidly in the period up to 1985, but the rate of growth would tend to decline over time. Another important implication of these projections is that the rates of growth in demand would be above average in Japan and in the United States; in Japan throughout the projection period, and in the United States through 1980. As a result, by 1980 Japan and the United States would account for three-quarters of the consumption in the world outside the tropical areas. This implies that demand prospects for tropical hardwood produced in the Asia-Pacific region in the next decade or so are especially favorable because of the latter's geographical proximity to the markets in Japan and the United States.

---

[12]Peck [38].
[13]ECE/FAO [7].
[14]See also FAO/ECE Timber Division [8].

V: Price Trends and Outlook for Tropical Hardwood in the Asia-Pacific Region

This chapter reviews the trends in prices and examines the future outlook for tropical hardwood prices in the Asia-Pacific region.

Price Trends

Because of the great variety of species and grades involved and the closed nature of the market, there is no one good indicator of the price of tropical hardwood logs. One way to observe the general trend in tropical hardwood prices would be to use the export (import) unit value — that is, the total value of logs exported (imported) divided by the total volume exported (imported). The export unit value of hardwood logs exported by all countries (developed as well as developing) has generally tended to rise slowly since the mid-1960s. On the basis of the FAO Forestry Department data, an index of export unit value of world hardwood log exports has been constructed as follows:

Period	Index
1955-59	100.0
1960-64	115.6
1965-69	116.1
1970	109.7

Source: Based on Table 5.1 and FAO [15], p. 142.

The average rate of increase between the latter half of the 1950s and that of the 1960s, based on the above index, is about 1.5 percent per annum.

Table 5.1: Export and Import Unit Values of Logs in World Trade 1960-70
(U.S. dollars per cubic meter)

	1960	1961	1962	1963	1964	1965	1966	1967	1968	1969	1970
Export Unit Value											
Hardwood (Nonconifer)											
World	25.1	23.8	24.6	24.4	23.3	23.9	25.0	24.9	24.4	23.5	23.0
Developed countries	37.0	36.3	38.0	40.3	39.4	50.9	43.8	43.2	49.6	51.1	49.7
Developing countries	23.6	22.4	23.1	23.0	22.0	21.8	23.6	23.4	22.8	22.1	21.6
Developing Africa	25.9	27.3	27.2	30.8	30.7	29.9	29.6	30.3	30.9	32.5	30.1
Developing Far East[1]	21.7	19.3	21.0	19.4	17.6	18.1	20.9	20.9	20.0	18.9	19.5
Developing Oceania[2]	54.7	43.3	33.0	22.5	16.1	16.8	15.0	16.1	15.0	14.1	15.7
Softwood (Conifer)											
World	18.2	18.6	20.2	16.1	17.0	18.1	18.5	18.5	20.8	22.4	23.6
Import Unit Value											
Hardwood (Nonconifer)											
World	35.2	34.3	34.7	35.4	35.0	35.3	35.0	35.0	35.6	37.2	36.7
Developed countries	35.9	34.5	35.3	36.0	36.7	37.6	37.3	37.0	38.2	39.0	38.0

[1]So-called East and Southeast Asia excluding Japan and CPEs
[2]Same as southwest Pacific islands

Source: FAO [20; 1970 ed.].

Table 5.2: C.I.F. Unit Values of Lauan and Apitong Logs[1] Imported by Japan, by Country of Origin, 1953-72

(U.S. dollars per cubic meter[2])

	Philippines	Sabah	Indonesia	All Sources[3]
1953	24.9	23.7	21.1	n.a.
1954	25.3	21.6	18.9	24.8
1955	28.8	25.0	19.3	28.4
1956	29.5	27.9	22.6	29.3
1957	24.3	22.2	22.8	24.0
1958	19.8	17.4	12.9	19.4
1959	22.4	20.6	13.6	22.0
1960	26.3	23.9	18.4	25.7
1961	24.5	22.4	18.1	23.8
1962	27.1	24.6	20.6	26.3
1963	27.9	25.1	19.6	27.3
1964	26.0	24.5	19.4	25.5
1965	27.4	25.3	19.8	26.6
1966	29.9	27.4	23.6	28.8
1967	32.0	29.3	24.9	30.7
1968	31.8	28.8	25.2	30.3
1969	31.7	29.8	28.3	30.2
1970	33.7	32.0	29.7	31.8
1971	35.0	32.3	30.6	32.3
1972	31.6	30.6	29.7	30.1

[1]Category 242-0310 in Japanese trade statistics
[2]Converted from Japanese yen figures at official exchange rate
[3]Include imports of lauans and apitongs from other sources such as West Malaysia, Sarawak

Source: Japan, Ministry of Finance [28; 1953-72 eds.].

On the other hand, the export unit value of hardwood logs exported from the "developing Asia-Pacific" region did not rise at all between 1960 and 1970.[1] However, this apparent stability in the price level, as measured by the unit value, of logs exported by the "developing Far East" region shows at best only one dimension of the price trends. The export unit value is by definition a *weighted* average of the prices of all kinds (species and grades) of logs exported from the region. As discussed earlier, the main exporters in this region have been the Philippines, Malaysia, and Indonesia and the main destination has been Japan. In the last two decades,

[1]See the export unit value series for the "developing Far East" and "developing Oceania" in Table 5.1. Although the Developing Far East includes Korea and Taiwan, which are not tropical, hardwood log exports from these countries are only of minor importance compared with those from the tropical Asia-Pacific region.

the relative weights of the three exporters in the region's total exports have been changing. In the early 1950s the Philippines was the only dominant source of log supply, but beginning around the late 1950s Malaysia (mainly Sabah and Sarawak) assumed an increasingly important position in the region's log exports. This trend continued throughout the 1960s. Indonesia became the third important exporter in the region around the mid-1960s and, as a result of the phenomenal increase in her log exports since, Indonesia became the largest exporter in the region in 1971. Since logs from Indonesia (mostly from Kalimantan) are less expensive than those from Sabah and Sarawak and logs from the latter sources are less expensive than those from the Philippines,[2] the changing relative shares of different sources of supply have tended to offset the upward trends observable in the price levels of logs exported from different countries as considered separately. Therefore, it is misleading to conclude on the basis of the apparent trends of export unit values that the prices of tropical hardwood logs exported from the Asia-Pacific region have not been rising.

Information is scanty on the long-term trend of the prices of logs exported by the Philippines, Malaysia, Indonesia, and others. That the prices of these logs in the most important market, Japan, have been rising can be seen from the import unit value calculated with respect to each country of origin separately (Table 5.2). Furthermore, the average cost of lauan (Dipterocarp) peeler logs to plywood manufacturers in Japan in selected years between 1952 and 1967 is as follows:

Year	$\#/m^3$
1952	$26.64
1955	$31.71
1960	$30.72
1965	$34.27
1967	$38.37

Source: Tuolumne Corporation [49].

Another available indicator, the Bank of Japan wholesale price index for "lauan" logs, also shows a definite upward trend as follows:

[2]See Table 5.2, which shows the import unit values (c.i.f. basis) of logs imported by Japan by country of origin since 1953. It may be noticed that there have been persistent differentials among the unit values of imports from different sources. Generally speaking, logs from the Philippines are preferred to logs from Sabah or Sarawak, which in turn are preferred to logs from Kalimantan (the Indonesian part of Borneo). Hence the price differentials.

Year	Index
1965	100.0
1966	105.9
1967	114.1
1968	116.7
1969	120.2

It must be noted that, generally speaking, because of the deterioration in the average quality of logs over the years, the cited data tend to underrepresent the true increases in prices.

The prices of tropical hardwood logs exported from Africa (which is the second-largest source next to the Asia-Pacific region) have also been rising. This is evident in the export unit value (1960-1969) in Table 5.1. It is also evident in the f.o.b. and c.i.f. prices of leading African species reported in *Marchés Tropicaux et Méditerranéens* during the 1956-1971 period. The prices of Lagos mahogany, obeche, sapelli, ilomba, okoume, makore, sipo, and others, expressed in terms of either the pound sterling or the CFA franc, all have risen in the last fifteen years at about 1.5 percent to 2.5 percent per annum.

Hardwood logs exported by developed countries are temperate hardwood. The prices of temperate hardwood also rose steadily during the relevant historical period. This rise is reflected in the export unit value of the developed countries. The prices of preferred hardwood species rose steadily in the developed countries. In the United States, for example, the prices of representative hardwood veneer logs rose in selected years as follows:

	(Dollars per 1,000 BF)			
Year	Maple (Wisconsin)	Walnut (Illinois)	White Oak (Illinois)	Black Walnut (Southern Indiana)
1953	90	147	124	n.a.
1956	105	228	79	n.a.
1961	120	284	99	250
1967	140	638	161	796
1970	153	750	275	1,250

Source: U.S. Department of Agriculture [53].

The marked increases in the prices of temperate hardwoods reflected the relative shortage of these species and were partly responsible for the increased demand for tropical hardwoods.

Price Outlook

What is the likely trend in the price of tropical hardwood in the Asia-Pacific region in the medium- to long-term future? The question can be answered upon examination of likely trends in demand and supply of tropical hardwood. The dominant end markets for the region's tropical hardwood are Japan and the United States, and the bulk of the tropical hardwood (including processed wood) imported by these two countries originally comes from the Asia-Pacific region (96 and 88 percent in Japan and the United States respectively as of 1970). If it is assumed that all of the projected demand in Japan and the United States should be met by the exports from the Philippines, Malaysia, and Indonesia only, then will there be sufficient volume of exportable supply of tropical hardwood in the latter three countries? This is the first question to be probed.

Exportable volume from the Philippines: The Philippines' sustainable annual hardwood log production, projected domestic consumption, and exportable volume of logs in 1975 and 1985, as estimated by the Tuolumne Corporation, are as follows:

	Million m^3(r)	
	1975	1985
Production	15.0	15.0
Domestic demand	3.0	4.3
Exportable volume	12.0	10.7

An increasing portion of the exportable volume is likely to be exported in processed form.

Exportable volume in Malaysia: Sustainable annual production, probable domestic consumption and exportable volume of log material in Malaysia as estimated by the Tuolumne study are as follows:

	Million m^3(r)	
	1975	1985
Sustainable log production	14.1	17.7
Domestic consumption	3.1	4.3
Exportable volume	11.0	13.4

Exportable volume of Indonesia: Annual log production and domestic consumption and exportable volume of log material in Indonesia have been projected by a recent World Bank agriculture sector mission as follows:

	Million m^3(r)		
	1972	1975	1985
Production	16.4	23.0	27.0
Domestic consumption	4.3	5.3	8.0
Exportable volume	12.1	17.7	19.0

Total exportable volume of logs in the Philippines, Malaysia, and Indonesia thus will be 40.7 and 43.0 million $m^3(r)$ in 1975 and 1985 respectively. On the other hand, combined total demand for tropical hardwood in Japan and the United States is projected to be 39.0 and 63.0 million $m^3(r)$ in 1975 and 1985 respectively. If it is assumed, however, that the relative shares of Southeast Asian timber in the totals imported by Japan and the United States are assumed to be maintained in the future, then the two countries would import 36.5 and 49.2 million $m^3(r)$ in 1975 and 1985 respectively. All this is summarized in the table below:

	Million $m^3(r)$	
	1975	1985
Exportable volume of the Philippines, Malaysia and Indonesia	40.7	43.0
Total import demand of Japan and the United States	39.0	63.0
Total demand of Japan and the United States for the timber of the above three suppliers if the current shares of various suppliers were maintained in the future	36.0	52.2

Turning for a moment to the probable demand by other areas, it may be assumed that, in 1975, other neighboring Pacific countries such as Canada, Australia, New Zealand, Korea, Taiwan, Hong Kong, and others will consume about 1.5 million $m^3(r)$ of tropical hardwood exported by the Philippines, Malaysia, and Indonesia. Currently Western Europe is taking about 2 million $m^3(r)$ from the three Asian exporters.[3] Demand for tropical hardwood in Europe in 1975 is expected to be about 2 million $m^3(r)$ higher than in 1968 (Table 4.1). It is a little doubtful whether African supply can expand sufficiently to meet all of this additional requirement. For the purpose of this paper, it is assumed then that tropical timber exports from the three Asian countries to Europe will increase to 2.5 million $m^3(r)$ by 1975. In addition, there are some minor exports to other countries not mentioned so far—South Africa, Middle Eastern countries, and the centrally planned countries. Exports to these countries are small and, in any case, will not increase enough to make a significant difference. Thus, demand by countries other than Japan and the United States for timber exports of the three Asian countries in 1975 may be assumed to be a little over 4 million $m^3(r)$.

It follows from the above analysis that, if likely demand by other countries is set aside, the Philippines, Malaysia, and Indonesia are likely to

---

[3]Excluding teak.

have just about sufficient exportable volume of tropical hardwood to meet the needs of the two largest traditional importers in 1975. It also follows that by 1985 a large part of the tropical timber demand in Japan and the United States will have to be satisfied by supplies coming from new sources other than the Philippines, Malaysia, and Indonesia. Even if demand by other importing countries did not increase materially between 1975 and 1985, perhaps an extra supply of 20 million $m^3(r)$ per annum will have to be found from new sources.

From the viewpoint of Japan and the United States, the most logical potential sources of additional tropical hardwood would be Papua/New Guinea and Latin America. Indochina cannot be expected to become a large exporter of tropical hardwood with or without political insecurity; Indochina might have an export capacity of up to 0.5 million $m^3(r)$ if there were no political insecurity.

The largest area in the non-Dipterocarp Pacific region, aside from Indonesia's West Irian, is Papua/New Guinea. Another large area of tropical hardwood forest reserves is in Latin America. However, there are two basic problems concerning these forest resources. One is that they contain very low volume of timber per unit area, yielding only about one-third the volume per hectare found in the typical forest of the Philippines. Another problem is that, as pointed out earlier, both of these areas have forests of quite diverse species mixture. The processing, handling, and marketing problems of such a varied mixture of species are much more difficult than those of the relatively uniform specie mixture in the Philippines, Malaysia, and Indonesia. With the added problem of serious lack of infrastructural facilities, therefore, the per unit cost of production of logs in these new areas is believed to be distinctly higher than that in, for example, the Philippines. As is clear from the preceding analysis, however, these new resources will have to be tapped after 1975.

The conclusion, therefore, is obvious. The prices of tropical hardwood could stay at current levels possibly until the mid-1970s but they are bound to rise sharply in the period beyond, barring drastic technological improvements in the production and transportation of tropical hardwood logs that would moderate the high costs of exporting massive volumes of logs from Papua/New Guinea and Latin America.

An important implication of the projected long-term rise in the prices of tropical hardwood logs would be that the timber resources that are located in the relatively more accessible areas, relatively rich in per-hectare volume and relatively uniform in species mixture, should command higher and higher economic rent over time. In fact, the Philippines, Malaysia, and Indonesia together have a virtual monopoly of relatively uniform (with respect to species), high density reserves of tropical hardwood.

Therefore, if the three countries *jointly* discourage the expansion of their total exports of logs *in the immediate future,* then they could in effect earn more income per unit of logs exported. Whether they could also improve their total foreign exchange earnings from log exports by exporting less quantity will depend on the relevant price elasticities of demand.

Annex 1: Projected Export Earnings from Timber of the Philippines, Malaysia and Indonesia, 1980

Reference was made at the outset of Chapter I to the projected export earnings from timber of the Philippines, Malaysia, and Indonesia for the year 1980. Annex Table 1.1 shows the volume and value of the timber exports from the countries in 1968 (actual as reported by FAO) and in 1980 (projected by the World Bank). The projected total roundwood equivalent volume of exports from the Philippines and Malaysia is based on the estimates given in the Tuolumne Corporation [49]. The breakdown of the total volume by product types was done by the present author somewhat arbitrarily, taking into account the product-by-product projections made in Sycip, Gorres, Velayo & Co. [47] and the Tuolumne Corporation [49]. The volume projections for Indonesia are based on the estimates made by the recent World Bank agriculture sector mission to Indonesia. The value projections are based on the assumption that the prices of logs, sawnwood, plywood, and veneers would increase respectively at the following annual rates: 4 percent (logs), 3 percent (sawnwood) and zero (plywood and veneers).

Annex Table 1.1: Estimated Growth of Timber Exports from the Philippines, Malaysia, and Indonesia, 1968 and 1980

	1968			1980 (Projected)	
	Volume		Value	Volume	Value
	million m³	million m³(r)	million $	million m³(r)	million $
The Philippines					
Total	n.a.	8.7	203	11.0	480
logs	7.5	7.5	170	2.0	70
sawnwood	0.10	n.a.	6	4.0	190
veneer	0.22	n.a.	8	included in plywood	
plywood	0.24	n.a.	19	5.0	220
Malaysia					
Total	n.a.	12.9	240	13.0	560
logs	10.51	10.51	179	3.0	80
sawnwood	1.20	n.a.	52	5.0	170
veneer	0.02	n.a.	2	included in plywood	
plywood	0.07	n.a.	8	5.0	310
Indonesia					
Total	n.a.	1.89	54	19.0	750
logs	1.88	1.88	53	10.0	300
sawnwood	0.01	n.a.	1	4.0	140
veneer	—	—	—	included in plywood	
plywood	—	—	—	5.0	310
The Three Countries					
Total	n.a.	23.5	497	43.0	1,790
logs	19.9	19.9	403	15.0	450
processed wood	n.a.	3.6	94	28.0	1,340

Source: 1968 data—FAO [20; 1969-70 eds.]; 1980 data—World Bank.

Annex 2: Import Duties on Tropical Wood Products in Developed Countries

Import duties on processed wood products are generally high in major importing countries, while logs are in most cases imported by these countries duty-free. Of particular importance to the tropical Asia-Pacific countries are the tariff structures on wood and wood products in Japan and the United States. Both Japan and the United States currently have a so-called tariff escalation in forest products (Annex Tables 2.1 and 2.2).

Generally speaking, products of higher degrees of processing have higher import duties in Japan and the United States although the circumstances are generally similar in other major developed countries as well (Annex Tables 2.3 and 2.4). Thus, the "effective rates of protection" on processed wood products in the developed countries are much higher than the "nominal rates of protection" would indicate. For instance, in the case of Japan, log raw material accounts for about 80 percent of the production cost of sawnwood and about 60 percent to 70 percent of that of plywood. Consequently, the effective rates of protection on sawmilling and plywood manufacturing activities in Japan are roughly 40 percent and 35 percent to 40 percent respectively. Similarly, the "effective rates of protection" are much higher than the "nominal rates of protection" on timber processing activities in the United States.

That the high import duties on processed products in the developed countries have had an important role to play is evidenced by the fact that exports of plywood from the Philippines to the United States had expanded up to a point in the mid-1960s and then could not continue to expand despite the continued rapid growth of the major market, the United States. The Laurel Langley Agreement provided for preferential tariffs on products coming from the Philippines to the United States. But, the preferential edges have been reduced every two years, and this obviously has been reducing the competitive edge which the Philippines has had in the U.S. plywood import market over other suppliers such as Korea and Taiwan. In the case of West Malaysia and, to a lesser extent, Sarawak it has been possible to export a considerable volume of sawnwood to the United Kingdom. This is at least partly due to the Commonwealth preference. Import duties on processed products, therefore, do affect the developing countries' manufacture exports. On the other hand, it is equally significant that, despite the high import duties in the United States, plywood exports of Korea and Taiwan to the United States have expanded tremendously — indeed overtaking the previous positions held by the Philippines and Japan in the U.S. import market. Therefore, the problem of the Philippine plywood exports is not solely due to the high import duties in the developed countries.

Under the UNCTAD scheme of Generalized Preferences, the EEC, the United Kingdom, several other European countries, and the United States, as well as a few other developed countries, made offers of duty-free access to manufactures and semimanufactures originating in developing countries, including most of wood products such as sawnwood, veneer sheets, and plywood. These offers, however, are subject to safeguard mechanisms of tariff quotas or escape clauses.

Japan's offer was to grant in principle duty-free entry to all manufactured and semimanufactured goods. It excludes, however, plywood and blockboard from preferential treatment, and offers only a 50 percent reduction of the GATT duties on the following items: sawnwood of Lauan, keruing, mersawa and other Dipterocarpacae family (mostly woods originating in the Philippines, Malaysia and Indonesia); and veneer sheets to be used for plywood. The Japanese offer includes the safeguard mechanism of tariff quotas very similar to that included in the EEC offer, the only significant deviation from the EEC plan being that the supplementary quota in the Japanese plan would be equal to 10 percent (as opposed to the 5 percent in the case of the EEC) of the imports from the nonbeneficiaries in the latest year.

A number of developed countries implemented their preferential arrangements for developing countries as follows:

EEC Member States .... July 1, 1971
Japan .... August 1, 1971
Norway .... October 1, 1971
Denmark .... January 1, 1972
Finland............... January 1, 1972
Ireland............... January 1, 1972
New Zealand........ January 1, 1972
Sweden............. January 1, 1972
United Kingdom .... January 1, 1972
Czechoslovakia...... February 28, 1972
Switzerland .... March 1, 1972
Austria............. April 1, 1972

Canada and the United States had not implemented their offers as of December 1973.

Annex Table 2.1: Tariff Rates on Selected Forest Products in Japan

	B.T.N.[1]	Item	Ad Valorem Rates
1.	44.03	Logs	free
2.	44.04	Sawnwood	
		Dipterocarpacea	10%
		other hardwoods	free
3.	44.14	Veneer sheets	
		tropical hardwoods	
		(except teak)	15%
		Teak	free
4.	44.15	Plywood	
		hardwood	20%
		softwood	17%
5.	44.18	Reconstituted wood	15-20%

[1]Here and elsewhere, Brussells Tariffs Classification
Source: Brussels International Customs Tariffs Bureau [4; no. 28], pp. 107-17.

Annex Table 2.2: U.S. Tariff Rates on Selected Forest Products
(percent ad valorem or equivalent)

	Item	Before 1968	After 1972
1.	Logs	free	free
2.	Sawn hardwood	0.8—1.1	0[1]
3.	Veneer		
	Southeast Asian species[2]	10	10
4.	Softwood plywood		
	Parana pine	40	20
	other species	20	20
5.	Hardwood plywood		
	Southeast Asian species[2]	20	20
	Spanish cedar	40	12.5
	others	15-20	7.5-10
6.	Particleboard	12-20	6-10

[1]Excluding Philippine mahogany, boxwood, Japanese maple, and Japanese white oak
[2]Lauans, bagtikan, meranti, red seraya, and white seraya
Source: U.S. Tariff Commission [55], pp. 89-103.

Annex Table 2.3: EEC Common Tariffs on Selected Forest Products

B.T.N.		Percentage		
		1968	1971	1972
4403 4404 4405	1. Wood in the Rough Logs or Sawn	Free	Free	Free
4413	2. Prepared Wood Planed and Grooved	8	6	5
4414	3. Veneer Sheets	8	7.2	7
4415	4. Plywood, Blockboard, and Laminboard (Wood plus Bonding only)	13.6	13.2	13
4418	5. (Particle Board, etc.) Reconstituted Wood	12.6	12.2	12

Source: Brussels International Customs Tariffs Bureau [4; no. 14], pp. 173-74.

Annex Table 2.4: U.K. External Tariffs[1] on Selected Forest Products, Prior to Joining the EEC

B.T.N.		Percentage		
		1969	1971	1972
4403 4404 4405	1. Wood in the Rough Logs or Sawn	Free	Free	Free
4413	2. Prepared Wood Planed and Grooved but not further manufactured	8	7	5
4414	3. Veneer	8	7	5
4415	4. Plywood (Wood plus Bonding only)	8	7	5
4418	5. Reconstituted Board	19	18	15

[1]Applicable to countries other than the members of EFTA and the Commonwealth

Source: Brussels International Customs Tariffs Bureau [4; no. 2], pp. 185-90.

Annex 3: Tropical Timber Bureau

One form of possible global action which merits support is a Tropical Timber Bureau. The idea emerged in 1966 between UNCTAD and FAO, which jointly convened working parties in 1966 and 1968. They stressed that "a major obstacle to increasing the flow of processed forest products was the lack of effective contracts between producers and consumers" and recommended the establishment of a Tropical Timber Bureau. The two international agencies then proposed in 1969 that UNDP support the initial period of such a bureau. UNDP will finance tentative establishment of a Tropical Timber Bureau for eventual global participation by interested countries.

The envisaged primary functions of a Tropical Timber Bureau are: to establish and strengthen regular contacts between producers and consumers; to expand the raw material basis of tropical timber trade by helping to bring new forest areas into production and by supporting actions to secure consumer acceptance of secondary and hitherto little used species in order to ensure conservation and improved management of tropical forest resources and soils; and to increase the imports of sawn timber, plywood, and other processed goods by the developed countries and to reduce the proportion of roundwood logs in tropical timber trade systematically. A Tropical Timber Bureau, if conceived and organized properly, could be an effective means of promoting tropical hardwood exports of developing countries including those in the Asia-Pacific region.

68

Statistical Appendix

Table A.1:   Production of Tropical Hardwood Logs, by Major Producing Countries, 1954-71

Table A.2:   Exports of Tropical Hardwood Sawnwood, by Major Countries, 1962-71

Table A.3:   Plywood: Production, Exports, Imports, and Apparent Consumption in Japan, 1956-70

Table A.4:   Plywood Exports of Japan, Quantity, Value, and Unit Value, 1955-72

Table A.5:   Share of Imported Wood in Wood Consumption in Principal Uses in Japan, 1962 and 1969

Table A.6:   Supply of Pulpwood in Japan, by Species and by Source, 1969

Table A.7:   Exports of Hardwood Plywood and Imports of Hardwood Logs by Korea and Taiwan, 1957-69

Table A.8:   U.S. Imports of Hardwood Veneer, by Country or Region of Origin, Selected Years, 1950-72

Table A.9:   Estimated U.S. Imports of Tropical Hardwood, by Product Category, 1968 (Actual), 1975, 1980, and 1985

Table A.10:   Imports of Tropical Hardwood Logs and Sawnwood by Seven Major Countries in Europe, by Regions and Countries of Origin, 1968

Table A.11:   Europe's Net Imports and Estimated Consumption of Tropical Hardwoods in 1965

Table A.12:   End-Uses for Tropical Hardwood in Europe in the Mid-1960s

Table A.13:   End-Use of Sawnwood in Japan by Species Group, 1967

Table A.14:   End-Use Pattern for Plywood in Japan, 1964

Table A.15:   Plywood Production and Capacity in Major Exporting Countries in Asia, 1969

Table A.16:   Prices of Tropical Hardwood Logs, Selected Species, f.o.b. Ivory Coast, 1956-73

Table A.17:   Unit Values of U.S. Imports of Philippine Hardwood Plywood, by Countries of Origin, 1953-72

Table A.18:   Price of Lauan Logs in Tokyo

Table A.19:   Price of Lauan Plywood in Tokyo

Table A.1: Production of Tropical Hardwood Logs, by Major Producing Countries, 1954-71
(unit: 1,000 m³(r))

	1954	1955	1956	1957	1958	1959	1960	1961
Tropical Latin America								
Costa Rica	n.a.	291	302	312	323	335	354	371
Cuba	128	113	85	138	130	145	155	180
Guatemala	185	113	125	112	187	225	225	225
Brazil	10,100	10,300	10,600	9,300	9,740	9,065	8,500	7,500
Colombia	2,020	2,130	2,160	2,180	2,180	2,180	2,180	2,180
Ecuador	n.a.	520	544	567	700	795	800	730
Paraguay	267	280	348	370	390	350	350	350
Venezuela	216	244	215	274	269	266	276	267
Tropical Africa								
Cameroon	322	350	353	355	373	352	345	394
Congo (Brazzaville)	n.a.	240	241	290	340	366	433	389
Congo (Kinshasa)	807	793	813	828	776	703	575	550
Equatorial Guinea	152	149	128	189	196	282	296	306
Gabon	1,150	1,339	1,307	1,477	1,653	1,616	1,748	1,600
Ghana	1,100	1,139	1,253	1,387	1,492	1,756	1,834	1,662
Ivory Coast	300	323	413	478	630	720	998	1,304
Madagascar	n.a.	53	94	83	123	160	165	170
Mozambique	n.a.	n.a.	n.a.	n.a.	n.a.	n.a.	n.a.	350
Nigeria	750	925	750	825	1,000	1,250	1,332	1,229
Tropical Asia								
Burma	1,205	1,261	1,319	1,544	1,289	951	1,365	1,600
India	2,365	2,489	2,653	2,696	2,703	—	3,480	2,884
Indonesia	3,889	3,887	3,896	3,952	3,505	3,591	3,947	3,944
West Malaysia	1,313	1,568	1,688	1,623	1,631	1,667	2,250	2,214
Sabah	521	615	765	949	1,149	1,557	2,142	2,607
Sarawak	452	643	623	676	650	863	1,163	1,189
Philippines	3,271	3,513	4,161	4,451	4,710	5,298	5,892	6,478
Thailand	1,715	1,696	1,558	1,638	1,771	1,279	1,345	1,337
New Guinea & Papua	75	105	137	131	140	146	117	206

*Unofficial figure
[1]Figures for the preceding year

Source: FAO [20; 1966-71 eds.]; FAO [18].

1962	1963	1964	1965	1966	1967	1968	1969	1970	1971
383	374	374	398	428	428	428	428	*718	*763
n.a.	449	449	449	449	449	39	39	31	*34
n.a.	400	400	400	400	400	400	400	*400	*400
5,900	5,190	5,650	10,200	10,770	8,000	8,370	8,530	8,885	*9,255
n.a.	n.a.	2,180	2,100	2,100	2,100	2,200	2,400	*3,740	*3,880
801	803	815	959	1,070	1,100	1,160	1,163	1,160	1,160
n.a.	n.a.	350	573	629	1,244	850	850	1,028	1,028
287	319	408	440	452	448	462	415	437	470
398	420	476	475	434	589	640	640	*750	*820
456	520	635	612	691	691	850	820	801	801[1]
425	454	425	425	450	450	488	488	*540	*560
377	421	436	412	463	500	500	530	*550	*550
1,441	—	1,441	1,261	1,498	1,531	1,639	1,835	*2,117	*2,117[1]
1,637	1,614	1,458	1,594	1,389	1,342	1,389	1,595	1,565	1,565[1]
1,454	1,820	2,249	2,554	2,608	2,788	3,266	3,266	*3,461	*3,883
180	165	165	395	445	500	710	712	1,005	1,096
n.a.	n.a.	440	460	460	350	350	350	*310	*320
1,119	n.a.	1,319	1,367	1,416	1,359	1,082	1,262	*1,400	*1,400
1,419	n.a.	1,419	1,419	1,552	1,817	1,731	1,728	1,737	1,722
n.a.	n.a.	2,884	2,884	4,801	4,801	3,120	3,120	*5,020	*5,200
4,023	4,065	4,065	4,065	4,065	4,065	5,515	5,810	*7,244	*10,661
2,312	2,698	2,981	3,284	3,791	4,185	5,064	5,328	*7,420	*7,920
2,783	3,447	3,562	4,153	5,971	5,674	5,892	6,075	6,546	6,941
1,360	1,700	1,844	2,306	2,986	3,599	4,233	4,243	4,692	3,916
6,772	7,536	8,700	8,490	7,395	9,954	11,089	11,472	*12,700	*11,600
1,412	1,724	1,866	2,496	2,121	2,330	2,546	2,527	*2,655	*2,725
213	270	357	462	474	623	637	332	436	645

Table A.2: Exports of Tropical Hardwood Sawnwood, by Major Countries, 1962-71
(unit: 1,000 m³(s))

	1962	1963	1964	1965	1966	1967	1968	1969	1970	1971
Tropical Africa										
Angola	n.a.	20.2	19	21	34.4	22.9	15.1	18.6	16.9	15.7
Congo (Kinshasa)	35.1	35.1	41	41	36.6	30.6	36.1	33.0	36.2	36.2²
Ghana	264.0	236.9	252	230	205.0	189.5	215.1	219.1	240.9	240.9²
Ivory Coast	48.0	56.2	96	153	182.0	183.1	188.1	200.0	182.9	163.1
Mozambique	65.2	71.9	106	112	91.3	88.0	88.0	79.8	86.1	66.6
Nigeria	66.2	77.4	87	82	74.3	52.5	59.5	66.2	47.4	38.6
Tropical Asia										
Burma	99.0	n.a.	99	225	113.8	102.6	100.4	121.9	115.5	109.0
Taiwan	39.7	39.4	44	42	47.2	53.9	54.0	51.9	n.a.	n.a.
West Malaysia	388.7	487.9	448	462	479.0	571.3	843.4	860.6	1,029.6	1,023.8
Singapore	1	1	338	402	472.4	434.0	556.1	719.7	720.6	649.8
Sarawak	182.6	207.6	261	271	221.6	275.0	310.8	304.6	314.8	281.6
Philippines	122.7	115.4	84	116	112.5	103.5	102.5	167.6	199.9	201.7
Thailand	93.7	96.0	109	90	67.2	45.0	34.6	37.9	37.9	62.2
Tropical Latin America										
Nicaragua	20.8	n.a.	9.4	18	25.2	21.0	20.5	13.9	11.4	12.2
Brazil	20.1	29.6	44.0	65	71.2	76.0	82.2	109.3	147.2	160.9
Colombia	32.7	49.2	8.3	44	47.2	55.0	104.2	150.2	157.2	122.0
Ecuador	12.8	6.8	34.0	13	39.9	63.3	62.1	62.9	62.5	65.2
Paraguay	26.2	12.5	39.0	45	38.5	28.6	45.2	83.7	86.4	84.1

[1]Included in West Malaysia

[2]Year 1970

Source: FAO [18]; FAO [20; 1962-71 eds.].

Table A.3: Plywood: Production, Exports, Imports and Apparent Consumption in Japan, 1956-70

(unit: million m²)

	Production	Exports	Imports	Apparent Consumption
1956-58[1]	270	78	0	192
1961-63[1]	519	87	0	432
1965	657	96	0.1	561
1966	775	94	0.4	681
1967	944	84	5.3	865
1968	1,186	106	0.9	1,081
1969	1,473	98	6.6	1,382
1970	1,764	81	63.8	1,747

[1]Annual averages

Source: Production, Ministry of Agriculture & Forestry Exports & Imports; Ministry of Finance; 1956-58, Sumito Ginko [46]; 1961-63, Rinya Kosaikai [42]; 1965-69, Shigesawa [43]; 1970, Japan, Ministry of Agriculture and Forestry [31; 8(4):5-20].

Table A.4: Plywood Exports of Japan, Quantity, Value[1] and Unit Value, 1955-72

	Lauan Plywood			Domestic Species Plywood			Specialty Plywood[2]			All Plywood	
	Quantity million m²	Value billion yen	Unit Value yen/m²	Quantity million m²	Value billion yen	Unit Value yen/m²	Quantity million m²	Value billion yen	Unit Value yen/m²	Quantity million m²	Value billion yen
1955	50.4	9.99	198	8.1	3.16	391	—	—	—	58.5	13.15
1956	52.0	10.32	198	13.1	5.08	386	—	—	—	65.1	15.39
1957	65.9	13.26	201	16.2	6.56	406	—	—	—	82.0	19.82
1958	69.7	13.62	195	16.5	6.37	387	—	—	—	86.1	19.99
1959	86.7	19.18	221	19.7	8.34	424	—	—	—	106.3	27.52
1960	68.6	13.61	198	19.8	8.93	451	—	—	—	88.4	22.53
1961	67.7	13.97	206	18.5	7.15	386	—	—	—	86.2	21.12
1962	67.7	15.23	225	21.8	9.10	417	—	—	—	89.5	24.33
1963	58.2	12.03	207	27.2	11.90	437	—	—	—	85.4	23.93
1964	49.9	8.74	175	25.2	10.79	428	14.9	5.10	341	90.1	24.63
1965	52.7	8.24	156	25.1	9.03	360	19.0	6.15	323	96.8	23.42
1966	44.6	7.31	164	25.4	10.12	399	24.4	9.17	376	94.3	26.60
1967	34.2	5.89	172	27.0	10.37	384	23.1	8.50	369	84.3	24.76
1968	44.8	7.95	177	33.9	14.49	427	27.5	11.06	402	106.2	33.50
1969	30.9	5.39	174	34.0	14.38	423	33.4	13.54	405	98.3	33.31
1970	20.6	4.07	197	30.5	11.20	368	29.2	11.58	396	80.3	26.85
1971	14.0	2.66	190	30.7	12.98	423	37.0	14.34	387	81.7	29.98
1972	2.3	0.44	194	33.3	14.2	427	32.0	12.70	397	67.6	27.38

[1]f.o.b. value
[2]Category created in 1964
Source: Japan, Ministry of Finance [28; 1955-72 eds.].

74

Table A.5: Share of Imported Wood[1] in Wood Consumption in Principal Uses in Japan, 1962 and 1969

(percentages)

Uses	1962	1969
Sawnwood	17.5	49.2
Pulpwood[2]	8.5	27.6
Plywood	85.2	92.4
Pitprops	—	—
Poles	2.5	13.5
Pilings and posts	37.8	38.8

[1]Includes all imported softwood and hardwood
[2]Includes wood chips, wood wastes, and residues used for pulping as well as imported woodpulp (in roundwood equivalent)

Source: Japan, Ministry of Agriculture and Forestry [30].

Table A.6: Supply of Pulpwood in Japan, by Species and by Source, 1969

(unit: 1,000 m³(r))

	Domestic Supply	Imports	Total
Softwood	6,710	3,719	10,429
roundwood	2,435	68	2,503
wood chips	4,275	3,651	7,926
Hardwood	13,702	560	14,262
roundwood	4,435	272	4,707
wood chips	9,267	288	9,555
Total	20,412	4,279	24,691
roundwood	6,870	340	7,210
wood chips	13,542	3,939	17,481

Source: Japan, Ministry of International Trade and Industry [32], pp. 9-11.

Table A.7: Exports of Hardwood Plywood and Imports of Hardwood Logs by Korea and Taiwan, 1957-69

	Unit	1957	1958	1959	1960	1961	1962	1963	1964	1965	1966	1967	1968	1969
Korea, Republic of														
log imports	1,000 m³	102.5	118.0	173.7	222.6	316.8	481.5	385.4	251.0	603.0	1,096.6	1,493.8	2,435.8	2,422.0
plywood exports	1,000 m³	—	—	0.8	2.4	14.2	15.2	46.7	151.6	169.6	276.6	311.4	600.0	708.6
Taiwan														
logs: gross imports	1,000 m³	91.2	128.8	137.6	161.1	168.0	276.0	446.5	562	625	691.9	899.7	1,090.1	1,193.3
logs: net imports	1,000 m³	90.0	127.2	106.2	160.8	158.2	267.7	444.5	561	624	687	895.7	1,088.4	1,190.0
plywood exports	1,000 m³	2.0	14.3	16.4	19.7	51.8	72.5	133.4	208.4	222.2	260.8	247.7	396.6	595.8
Korea + Taiwan														
log imports, gross	1,000 m³	194	247	311	384	485	758	832	813	1,228	1,789	2,394	3,525.9	3,615.3
plywood exports	1,000 m³	2	14	17	22	66	88	180	360	392	537	559	996.6	1,304.4
plywood exports	1,000 m³(r)	5	33	40	51	152	202	414	828	901	1,236	1,286	2,292	3,000.0

Source: FAO, [18]; FAO [20; 1964-70 eds.].

Table A.8: U.S. Imports of Hardwood[1] Veneer, by Country or Region of Origin, Selected Years, 1950-72[2]

(unit: million m[2], surface measure)

	Latin America	Asia (excluding Japan)			Africa	Total Tropical[3]	Canada	Temperate Region			World Total
		Philippines	Other	Total				Europe	Other	Total	
1950	0.2	—	—	—	0.3	0.5	32.4	0.7	—	33.1	33.6
1954-56[4]	0.5	4.0	0.1	4.1	2.8	7.4	56.4	0.3	0.3	57.0	64.4
1959-61[4]	2.2	18.7	0.2	18.9	7.8	28.9	49.0	2.1	7.8	57.8	86.7
1965	6.2	49.0	14.4	63.4	20.4	90.1	79.2	4.1	0.5	83.8	173.9
1966	9.0	48.6	17.4	66.0	19.5	94.5	73.7	2.8	0.4	76.8	171.3
1967	13.1	42.0	11.6	53.6	25.2	91.9	72.1	2.6	0.4	75.1	167.0
1968	18.6	56.7	20.8	77.5	25.7	121.8	77.9	2.4	0.4	80.7	202.5
1969	14.2	62.4	15.0	77.4	11.9	103.5	66.3	2.1	0.6	69.0	172.5
1970	17.8	42.8	9.8	52.6	13.7	84.0	62.5	2.4	0.3	65.2	149.2
1971	20.1	54.9	19.9	74.8	13.3	108.2	78.2	2.2	0.4	80.8	189.1
1972	28.1	76.4	37.4	113.8	14.3	129.9	97.7	2.8	0.1	100.6	258.6

1Includes mixed species not classified as hardwoods or softwoods for the years 1950-59
2Data may not add to totals because of rounding
3Includes some nontropical countries
4Three-year averages

Source: U.S. Department of Agriculture [53],p. 82; U.S. Dept. of Commerce [54, 1972 ed.].

Table A.9: Estimated U.S. Imports of Tropical Hardwood, by Product Category, 1968 (Actual), 1975, 1980, and 1985

Product	Unit	1968	Projected 1975	Projected 1980	Projected 1985
plywood & veneer	million m² (9.5 mm basis)	240	400	510	550
	million m³(r)	5.4	9.1	11.5	12.5
sawnwood	million m³(s)	0.44	0.86	1.4	1.8
	million m³(r)	0.8	1.6	2.6	3.3
logs	million m³(r)	0.2	0.2	0.2	0.2
Total	million m³(r)	6.4	10.9	14.3	16

Source: Author's projections; see Chapter IV, "Demand in the United States."

Table A.10: Imports of Tropical Hardwood Logs and Sawnwood by Seven Major Countries in Europe[1], by Regions and Countries of Origin, 1968

Region of Origin	Logs 1,000 m³(r)	Sawnwood 1,000 m³(s)	Sawnwood 1,000 m³(r)
Latin America	42	28	51
Africa[2] of which	4,580	469	854
Gabon	990	—	—
Ghana	446	163	297
Ivory Coast	2,066	165	300
Asia-Pacific[3] of which	340	670	1,220
Malaysia	125	525	955
Total	4,964	1,169	2,128

[1]U.K., France, Federal Republic of Germany, Italy, Netherlands, Belgium-Luxembourg, and Denmark. These countries accounted for 85 percent of total imports of tropical hardwood in Europe in 1965
[2]All Africa excluding South Africa
[3]All Asia excluding Japan plus the developing Oceania
Source: FAO [20; 1970 ed.].

Table A.11: Europe's Net Imports and Estimated Consumption of Tropical Hardwoods in 1965
(unit: million m³(r))

	Net Imports Volume	Net Imports Percent	Consumption Volume	Consumption Percent	Conversion in Europe Volume
Logs	5.4	69	0.2	2	
Sawnwood	1.9	25	3.2-3.6	41-46	1.3-1.7
Plywood	0.4	5	2.6-2.8	33-36	2.2-2.4
Veneers	0.05	1	1.4-1.6	18-21	1.3-1.5
Total	7.8	100	7.8	100	

Source: FAO/ECE Timber Division [8], p. 31.

Table A.12: End-Uses for Tropical Hardwood in Europe in the Mid-1960s

	Furniture	Construction[1]	Transport	Ship and boat building[2]	Packaging[3]	Hydraulic Works	Other[4]	Total
			Approximate percentage					
Germany, Federal Republic	50-55	36-40	2	2	—	1-2	5-7	100
United Kingdom	40	40	3-5	5-7.5	—	—	7.5-10	100
France	40	36-41.5	2-3	5-6	1.5-2	—	7-10	100
Netherlands	40	27	3	2-3	4-5	17	5-7	100
Belgium	45	35	2-2.5	4-5	2	—	8-11	100
Switzerland	40	47-53	1-2	1	1-2	—	8-11	100
Sweden	40	35-40	3-5	10	—	—	8-10	100
Norway	35-40	32-33	2	20	—	—	5-7	100
Weighted average, 8 countries	43-45	37-40	2-3	4-5	—	—	9-12	100

[1]Includes door-making and parquet
[2]Including repairs
[3]May include shuttering in some countries
[4]Where percentage is not shown for "packaging" or "hydraulic works," this is included under "other"
Source: FAO/ECE Timber Division [8], p. 35.

Table A.13: End-Use of Sawnwood in Japan by Species Group, 1967
(unit: percent)

	Total all species groups	Softwood				Hardwood			
		Total	Domestic	U.S.	USSR	Total	Domestic	Tropical	Other
All uses	100	83	67	14	2	17	4	12	1
Construction	100	92	77	14	1	8	1	7	—
Civil engineering	100	90	72	17	1	10	8	2	—
Packaging	100	71	59	10	2	29	10	18	1
Furniture	100	10	7	3	—	90	22	65	3
Shipbuilding	100	83	61	21	1	17	11	5	1
Joinery	100	49	21	23	5	51	15	33	3
Others	100	79	34	20	25	21	8	7	6

Source: Tuolumne Corporation [49], p. 124.

Table A.14: End-Use Pattern for Plywood in Japan, 1964

(unit: percent)

End-Use	Total	Lauan Plywood	Domestic Specie Plywood	Specialty Plywood
Construction	45.4	34.4	46.2	56.9
Furniture	13.2	13.0	28.5	11.1
Joinery	27.8	28.5	6.0	27.1
Shop fittings	5.8	6.1	8.3	1.3
Other	7.8	18.0	11.0	3.6
Total	100.0	100.0	100.0	100.0

Source: Tuolumne Corporation [49], p. 140.

Table A.15: Plywood Production and Capacity in Major Exporting Countries in Asia, 1969

	Production 1,000 m³	Capacity 1,000 m³/year	Capacity Utilization %
Philippines	455.0	952	48
West Malaysia	150.0	175	86
Sabah & Sarawak	12.2	19	64
Indonesia	6.6	10	66
Singapore[1]	5.1	65	78
Korea	652.0	1,060	62
Taiwan	498.0	565	88
Japan	5,890.0	7,180	82

[1]Singapore figures for 1968

Source: FAO Committee on Wood-Based Panel Products [19], country tables.

Table A.16: Prices of Tropical Hardwood Logs,[1] Selected Species, f.o.b. Ivory Coast, 1956-73

(unit: CFA Francs per cubic meter)

	Acajou (Kyaya)	Makore[2]	Niangon	Samba (Wama obeche)	Sipo (Utile)	Tiama	Sapelli[3]	Average Price of 7 species[4]	Exchange Rate CFA Francs/U.S.$
1956	6,475	6,919	7,019	4,125	6,863	4,531	6,306	6,034	n.a.
1957	6,156	6,938	6,625	4,000	6,250	4,375	6,113	5,780	n.a.
1958	7,000	7,881	7,638	4,375	7,313	5,406	6,950	6,652	246.85
1959	7,575	8,500	8,500	4,600	7,519	5,138	7,281	7,016	246.85
1960	9,750	9,250	8,625	5,650	8,125	5,781	8,594	7,968	246.85
1961	9,500	9,550	8,875	6,356	8,656	6,438	9,688	8,430	246.85
1962	9,000	9,375	9,125	6,375	8,625	6,625	9,250	8,339	246.85
1963	9,438	9,656	9,188	6,719	9,469	7,063	9,656	8,741	246.85
1964	10,188	10,250	9,750	6,625	10,875	7,375	9,750	9,259	246.85
1965	9,875	11,250	9,625	6,063	10,750	7,375	9,750	9,241	246.85
1966	9,625	11,763	8,938	5,938	10,750	7,094	9,375	9,069	246.85
1967	10,125	10,938	9,000	6,031	11,375	7,563	9,250	9,183	246.85
1968	10,219	11,313	9,188	6,250	13,500	8,313	10,375	9,880	246.85
1969	11,000	12,813	10,500	7,250	16,688	8,719	12,875	11,406	277.71
1970	9,781	14,250	10,250	6,969	14,656	8,438	11,938	10,897	277.71
1971	9,813	14,063	10,656	7,281	15,813	9,000	12,313	11,277	255.79
1972	12,063	14,000	12,313	7,825	20,375	11,125	13,250	12,993	255.79
1973[5]	22,500	22,500	20,750	12,500	38,250	18,500	23,750	22,679	234.51

[1]The average of the mid-month quotations for "loyal et marchand" grade for March, June, September, and/or nearby months
[2]Diameter 100 cm. and over
[3]f.o.b. Cameroon
[4]Simple arithmetic average
[5]The first half of the year

Source: "Cours des Products," weekly in [35; 1956-73, nos. 530-1455]; IMF [26; XVIII (1): 174-75]; IMF [26; XXVI (12): 27].

82

Table A.17 : Unit Values¹ of U.S. Imports of Philippine Hardwood Plywood, by Countries of Origin, 1953-72

(U.S.$ per 1,000 square feet)

	Actual Unit Values					Deflated² Unit Values		
	Philippines	Korea	Taiwan	Japan	All Countries	Philippines	Japan	All Countries
1953	(31.91)	—	(60.80)	62.51	68.92	36.43	71.36	78.68
1954	(79.09)	—	(40.44)	56.23	59.81	90.08	64.04	68.12
1955	(104.77)	—	(95.87)	62.36	66.73	118.92	70.78	75.74
1956	81.99	—	67.21	60.59	64.81	90.20	66.66	71.30
1957	66.82	—	38.24	62.73	65.24	71.39	67.02	69.70
1958	60.19	—	40.25	63.67	64.73	63.42	67.09	68.21
1959	68.94	54.14	48.35	70.96	70.61	72.49	74.62	74.25
1960	66.78	52.34	35.06	55.65	56.30	70.15	58.46	59.14
1961	55.75	43.39	43.31	55.25	52.92	58.81	58.28	55.82
1962	67.79	50.33	47.55	59.02	57.54	71.28	62.06	60.50
1963	62.94	46.32	40.04	54.28	51.55	66.39	57.26	54.38
1964	60.40	45.77	41.69	48.85	48.71	63.58	51.42	51.27
1965	58.61	43.50	40.50	42.68	45.22	60.50	44.05	46.67
1966	55.95	43.99	41.13	43.71	45.54	55.95	43.71	45.54
1967	50.22	42.94	40.03	46.73	44.38	50.07	46.59	44.25
1968	49.56	45.75	41.33	46.72	45.30	48.30	45.53	44.15
1969	52.96	45.80	42.51	45.28	45.89	49.63	42.44	43.01
1970	41.90	41.50	38.92	48.12	41.25	37.88	43.51	37.26
1971	42.07	42.81	39.98	47.63	42.03	36.89	41.73	36.81
1972	42.90	43.89	39.14	56.44	42.28	35.95	47.29	35.43

¹f.o.b. countries of origin
²Deflated by wholesale price index, 1966 = 100

Source: U.S. Bureau of the Census [52].

Table A.18: Price of Lauan Logs in Tokyo¹
(in thousand yen per m³)

	1963	1964	1965	1966	1967	1968	1969	1970	1971	1972	1973
January	13.2	11.8	11.0	13.0	13.3	15.0	14.0	14.0	16.0	12.6	14.8
February	13.2	11.8	12.0	13.3	13.5	15.0	14.0	14.6	16.0	12.9	19.1
March	13.3	11.5	12.3	13.3	13.8	15.0	14.0	15.0	16.0	13.3	19.7
April	13.3	11.0	12.8	13.1	13.8	15.0	14.0	15.0	16.0	13.2	18.8
May	13.6	10.6	12.8	13.3	14.0	15.0	14.0	15.6	15.9	13.0	16.3
June	13.5	10.6	12.8	13.3	14.0	15.0	14.0	16.0	15.5	12.4	14.7
July	13.0	10.5	12.8	13.3	14.0	14.0	14.0	16.0	15.1	11.8	14.9
August	12.5	10.5	12.8	13.3	14.0	14.0	14.0	16.0	15.0	11.8	16.8
September	12.2	10.4	13.0	13.3	14.5	14.0	14.0	16.0	14.5	11.9	18.7
October	11.8	10.4	13.0	13.3	15.0	14.0	14.0	16.0	14.4	11.9	20.8
November	11.7	10.6	13.0	13.3	15.0	14.0	14.0	16.0	13.6	11.9	21.4
December	12.0	11.0	13.0	13.3	15.0	14.0	14.0	16.0	13.2	13.1	27.0
Annual Average	12.8	10.9	12.6	13.26	14.16	14.5	14.0	15.6	15.1	12.5	18.6

¹Philippines, 3.6 meters or more times 60 centimeters, delivered Tokyo, importers' sales price to wholesalers, as of around the middle of the month

Source: "Major Quotations," in [36; 1963-72, nos. 1-569].

Table A.19: Price of Lauan Plywood in Tokyo[1]

(in yen per sheet)

	1963	1964	1965	1966	1967	1968	1969	1970	1971	1972	1973
January	320	250	220	215	300	275	295	330	311	270	454
February	330	255	220	230	305	275	295	340	310	283	548
March	330	236	230	260	305	280	305	355	310	290	586
April	330	236	230	260	295	285	305	393	310	284	550
May	320	233	230	270	290	285	305	420	310	270	429
June	305	234	215	270	280	280	305	420	280	270	370
July	285	232	215	270	280	280	300	408	260	270	400
August	280	230	215	275	275	290	299	396	272	279	488
September	275	228	215	280	280	290	302	386	294	273	590
October	275	228	215	280	280	300	305	362	262	315	580
November	275	230	215	290	285	300	310	324	250	325	544
December	275	228	215	290	285	295	320	318	270	379	643
Average	300	233	220	265	288	286	304	371	287	294	515

[1]3-Ply, extra, 91 centimeters times 182 centimeters times 4 millimeters, Tokyo wholesale, spot price, as of around the middle of the month

Source: "Major Quotations," in [36; 1963-72, nos. 1-569].

References

[1] [Arnold, J.E.M.] FAO Secretariat. "Expansion of Exports of Forest Products from Developing Countries." *UNASYLVA* 22 [1] (1968): 30-40 and 22 [2] (1968): 31-44.

[2] Balassa, B.A. "Industrial Policies in Taiwan and Korea." *Weltwirtschaftliches Archiv* 106 (1971): 55-77.

[3] Balassa, B.A. "The Structure of Protection in Industrial Countries and its Effects on the Exports of Processed Goods from Developing Countries." In UNCTAD, *The Kennedy Round Estimated Effects on Tariff Barriers,* pp. 187-217. (TD/6/Rev. 1) New York, 1968.

[4] Brussels International Customs Tariffs Bureau. *The International Customs Journal (Bulletin International des Douanes),* no. 28 (13th ed., 1972-73) *Japan;* no. 14 (3d ed., 1972-73) *European Economic Community;* no. 2 (26th ed., 1972-73) *Great Britain and Northern Ireland.*

[5] Chusho Kigyo Shinko Jigyodan [Small and Medium Business Development Foundation]. *Gohan Seizogyo Kosto Kaiseki* [Plywood industry, an analysis of cost]. Tokyo, 1971.

[6] Economic Committee for Europe/Food and Agriculture Organization. *Annual Forest Products Market Review: 1970 and up to October 1971,* Part II. Geneva, November 1971.

[7] Economic Committee for Europe/Food and Agriculture Organization. *European Timber Trends and Prospects, 1950-80, An Interim Review.* Vol. 1 Supplement 7 to *Timber Bulletin for Europe* XXI (May 1969).

[8]   Economic Committee for Europe/Food and Agriculture Organization, Timber Division. "Consumption of Tropical Hardwoods in Europe." *UNASYLVA* 21 [1] (1967): 31-38.

[9]   Economic Committee for Europe/Food and Agriculture Organization, Timber Division. *Timber Bulletin for Europe.* Published twice yearly, 1953-   .

[10]   Economic Commission for Latin America/Food and Agriculture Organization/UN Industrial Development Organization. "Prospects for Forest Industries Development in Latin America." Paper presented to the Regional Consultation on the Development of the Forest and Pulp and Paper Industries in Latin America, in Mexico City, May 1970. (FORIND 7, Paper IX) New York, February 1970.

[11]   Food and Agriculture Organization. *Agricultural Commodities — Projections for 1975 and 1985.* 2 vols. (CCP 67/3 rev.) Rome, 1967.

[12]   Food and Agriculture Organization. "A Reappraisal of the Outlook for the Future 1968 to 1980." Paper presented to the Third Session of the FAO Committee on Wood-Based Panel Products. (FOI: WPP/70/3.3) Rome, December 1970.

[13]   Food and Agriculture Organization. *Commodity Review and Outlook, 1971-72.* Rome, 1972.

[14]   Food and Agriculture Organization. *Provisional Indicative World Plan for Agricultural Development.* Vols. I and II. Rome, 1970

[15]   Food and Agriculture Organization. *The State of Food and Agriculture, 1969.* Rome, 1970.

[16]   Food and Agriculture Organization. *Timber Trends and Prospects in Africa.* Rome, 1967.

[17]   Food and Agriculture Organization. *World Demand for Paper to 1975.* Rome, 1960.

[18]   Food and Agriculture Organization. *World Forest Products Statistics. A Ten-Year Summary, 1954-63.* Rome, 1965.

[19]   Food and Agriculture Organization, Committee on Wood-Based Panel Products. *World Production Capacities, Plywood, Particle Board and Fibreboard, 1967-71.* Mimeographed (FOI: WPP/70/3.2) Rome, November 1970.

[20]   Food and Agriculture Organization. *Yearbook of Forest Products.* Published annually, 1950-

[21]   Food and Agriculture Organization. *Wood: World Trends and Prospects.* Rome, 1967.

[22]   Garnaut, R. "Policy for Timber Processing." *Bulletin of Indonesian Economic Studies* VII (November 1971): 144-46.

[23]   Hair, D. "Current and Prospective Trends in Imports of Hardwood Timber Products into the United States." In *Proceedings of the Conference on Tropical Hardwoods.* Syracuse, N.Y.: Syracuse University College of Forestry, 1969.

[24]   Hair, D. and Spada, B. "Hardwood Timber Resources of the United States." *UNASYLVA* 24 [4] (1970): 29-32.

[25]   Hair, D. and Ulrich, A.H. *The Demand and Price Situation for Forest Products, 1971-72.* U.S. Department of Agriculture Forest Service miscellaneous publication 1231. Washington, D.C.: U.S. Government Printing Office, 1972.

[26]   International Monetary Fund. *International Financial Statistics.* Published monthly.

[27]   Japan, Forestry Agency. *Mokuzai Jukyn To Mokuzai-Kogyo No Genkyo* [Supply and demand of timber and the current conditions of timber processing industries]. Tokyo, November 1971.

[28]   Japan, Ministry of Finance. *Japan Exports and Imports Commodity by Country.* Published annually.

[29]   Japan, Ministry of Agriculture and Forestry. *Basic Plan Regarding Forest Resource and Long Range Prospect Regarding Demand and Supply of Important Forest Products.* Tokyo, February 1973.

[30]   Japan, Ministry of Agriculture and Forestry. *Showa 45 Nendo Ringyo Hakusho* [Annual report on forestry for the year 1970]. Tokyo, April 1971.

[31]   Japan, Ministry of Agriculture and Forestry. *Gohan Tokei* [Statistics of plywood]. Published monthly.

[32]   Japan, Ministry of International Trade and Industry. *Yearbook of Pulp and Paper Statistics for 1969.* Tokyo, 1970.

[33]   Korea Productivity Center, Institute of Productivity Research. *The Analysis of Cost and Rate of Net Foreign Exchange Earnings of Korea Export Products.* Seoul, 1970.

[34]   Manning, C. "The Timber Boom with Special Reference to East Kalimantan." *Bulletin of Indonesian Economic Studies* VII (November 1971): 30-60.

[35]   *Marchés Tropicaux et Méditerranéens,* nos. 530-1455 (1956-73). Published weekly.

[36]   Nihon Keizai Shimbun [Japan Economic Journal]. *The Nihon Keizai Shimbun International Weekly Edition.* Published weekly.

[37]   Paterno, V.T. "Regional Cooperation in Timber Processing." *The Philippine Lumberman* XVII (December 1971): 6-10.

[38]   [Peck, T.J.] ECE/FAO Timber Division. "Trends and Prospects in the European Market for Forest Products." Paper read to the

Regional Poplar Congress, May 1973, at Wageningen, The Netherlands. Mimeographed.

[39] Power, J.H. and Sicat, G.P. *The Philippines: Industrialization and Trade Policies.* London: Oxford University Press, 1971.

[40] Pringle, S.L. "Hardwoods—World Supply and Demand (With Emphasis on Tropical Species)." *UNASYLVA* 23 [2] (1969): 24-33 and 23 [3] (1969): 34-39.

[41] Richardson, S.D. "The Availability of Supplies from Current Resources." Paper read to the Symposium on the Availability of Tropical Hardwoods, February 1970, at the University College of North Wales, Bangor. Mimeographed.

[42] Rinya Kosaikai. *Ryngyo Tokei Yoran [1970]*[Statistical handbook on forestry]. Tokyo, 1971.

[43] Shigesawa, S. "Plywood Industry in Japan." Paper read to FAO Committee on Wood-Based Panel Products Third Session, December 1970, at Rome. Mimeographed.

[44] Singh, Chandra. "Prospects for Hardwood Plywood Exports from Developing Countries, 1965-75." Mimeographed. Washington, D.C.: World Bank, 1968.

[45] Snape, R.H. "Trade in Processed Agricultural Products, with Special Reference to Sugar." In *Obstacles to Trade in the Pacific Area, Proceedings of the Fourth Pacific Trade and Development Conference,* ed. H.E. English and Keith A.J. Hay, pp. 121-41. Ottawa: Carleton University School of International Affairs, 1972.

[46] Sumitomo Ginko [Sumitomo Bank]. "Plywood Manufacturing in Japan." *Sumito Bank Review* VII, no. 6 (November-December 1967).

[47] Sycip, Gorres, Velayo and Company. "The Philippine Wood Industry in the Seventies." Multiclient study, mimeographed. Manila, 1971.

[48] The Tuolumne Corporation. "The Market Potential for West Irian Timber and Timber Products." Report to the Fund of the United Nations for the Development of West Irian, n.p., June 1969. Mimeographed.

[49] The Tuolumne Corporation. "Market Study for Forest Products from East Asia and the Pacific Region." Report to the Food and Agriculture Organization, San Francisco, July 1971. Mimeographed.

[50] Turnbang, J. and von Hegel, D. "Development of Forestry and Forest Industries in Asia." In *Asian Agricultural Survey,* Asian Development Bank, pp. 448-512. Seattle, Wash.: University of Washington Press, 1969.

[51]   United Nations Conference on Trade and Development. Intra-
        Regional Trade of Forest Products in Latin America (TD/B/C.2/
        A/ C2/22). Geneva, 1968.
[52]   U.S. Department of Commerce, Bureau of the Census. *U.S. Imports
        for Consumption and General Imports.* Published annually.
[53]   U.S. Department of Agriculture, Forest Service. *The Demand and
        Price Situation for Forest Products, 1970-71.* Forest Service
        miscellaneous publication no. 1195. Washington, D.C.: U.S.
        Government Printing Office, 1971.
[54]   U.S. Department of Commerce, Bureau of the Census. *U.S. Foreign
        Trade Imports TSU SA Commodity by Country.* Published annually.
[55]   U.S. Tariff Commission. *Tariff Schedules of the United States, Anno-
        tated (1971).* Washington, D.C.: U.S. Government Printing
        Office, 1971.
[56]   Westoby, J.C. "The Role of Forest Industries in the Attack on Eco-
        nomic Underdevelopment." *UNASYLVA* 16 [4] (1962):
        168-201.
[57]   World Bank, "Nigeria Agricultural Sector Mission Report."
        Mimeographed. Washington, D.C., 1971.